Congressional
Research
Service

The FHA Single-Family Mortgage Insurance Program: Financial Status and Related Current Issues

Katie Jones
Analyst in Housing Policy

December 21, 2012

Congressional Research Service

7-5700

www.crs.gov

R42875

Summary

The Federal Housing Administration (FHA) insures home mortgages made by private lenders against the possibility of borrower default. If the borrower does not repay the mortgage, FHA pays the lender the remaining principal amount owed. By insuring lenders against the possibility of borrower default, FHA is intended to expand access to mortgage credit to households, such as those with smaller downpayments or below-average credit histories, who might not otherwise be able to obtain a mortgage at an affordable interest rate or at all. FHA also traditionally plays a countercyclical role in the mortgage market. In other words, it generally insures more mortgages during periods when lenders and private mortgage insurers tighten their lending standards and reduce activity in response to market conditions, and it generally insures fewer mortgages at times when lenders and private mortgage insurers make mortgage credit more easily available.

When an FHA-insured mortgage goes to foreclosure, the lender files a claim with FHA for the remaining amount owed on the mortgage. Claims on FHA-insured loans have traditionally been paid out of an account, known as the Mutual Mortgage Insurance Fund (MMI Fund), that is funded through fees paid by borrowers, rather than through appropriations. However, if FHA were ever unable to pay claims that it owed, it can draw on permanent and indefinite budget authority with the U.S. Treasury to pay those claims without additional congressional action.

In recent years, increased default and foreclosure rates, as well as economic factors such as falling house prices, have contributed to an increase in expected losses on FHA-insured loans. This increase in expected losses has put pressure on the MMI Fund and reduced the amount of resources that FHA has on hand to pay for additional, unexpected future losses. This has led to concern that FHA may need to draw on its permanent and indefinite budget authority for funds from Treasury to hold in reserve to pay for these higher expected future losses, or, eventually, to pay insurance claims. An annual actuarial review of the MMI Fund released in November 2012 showed that, according to current estimates, FHA does not currently have enough funds on hand to cover all of its expected future losses on the loans that it currently insures. The results of this actuarial review heightened concerns that FHA could need funds from Treasury. However, whether FHA actually needs to draw funds from Treasury would be determined as part of the annual budget process, not by the actuarial review.

FHA faces an inherent tension between protecting its financial health and fulfilling its mission of expanding access to mortgage credit. In addition, the share of mortgages insured by FHA has increased in the past several years as the availability of mortgage credit has tightened, further contributing to this tension. FHA has recently proposed or implemented a number of changes to its single-family mortgage insurance program that are intended to minimize risk to the MMI Fund while still allowing FHA to support the mortgage market and expand access to affordable mortgages. These changes have included increasing the fees that it charges to borrowers for insurance, modifying its underwriting criteria, and taking steps to increase oversight of lenders who make FHA-insured loans. While many of these changes were made administratively by FHA, some involved congressional action. Congress has also weighed additional changes to FHA's programs, and has considered additional legislation aimed at protecting the financial health of the MMI Fund. An example of such a bill is the FHA Emergency Fiscal Solvency Act of 2012 (H.R. 4264), which passed the House of Representatives during the 112th Congress. An identical bill (S. 3678) has been introduced in the Senate.

Contents

Figures

Tables

Appendixes

Contacts

Introduction

The Federal Housing Administration (FHA) insures home mortgages made to individuals by private lenders. If the individual does not repay the mortgage and the home goes to foreclosure, FHA pays the lender the remaining amount that the borrower owes. FHA was established by the National Housing Act of 1934, in the aftermath of the Great Depression, and became part of HUD in 1965. The National Housing Act has been amended a number of times to allow FHA to insure a wider variety of mortgages than just mortgages on single-family homes, including mortgages on multifamily buildings, hospitals, and other health care facilities. This report only addresses FHA's traditional single-family mortgage insurance program, which insures mortgages to purchase or refinance single-family (one-to-four unit) homes with principal balances under a certain threshold. Except where otherwise specified, this report does not discuss FHA-insured reverse mortgages, although these mortgages are financed through the same insurance account as traditional FHA-insured single-family mortgages.[1]

This report begins with a brief overview of FHA's current role in the mortgage market. It then describes the financial status of the insurance fund that finances FHA-insured single-family mortgages, known as the Mutual Mortgage Insurance Fund, including its treatment in the federal budget and measures of its actuarial soundness. Finally, it outlines major changes that FHA has recently made or has proposed making to its single-family mortgage insurance program to address concerns about its financial stability, as well as additional changes considered by Congress. Although this report provides a description of FHA's current role in the mortgage market to provide context, it does not address ongoing debate about the appropriate role for FHA in the mortgage market going forward.

FHA's Role in the Mortgage Market

FHA is one of three government agencies that provide insurance or guarantees on certain home mortgages made by private lenders, along with the Department of Veterans Affairs (VA) and the United States Department of Agriculture (USDA).[2] FHA is the most broadly targeted of these federal mortgage insurance programs. Unlike VA- and USDA-insured mortgages, the availability of FHA-insured mortgages is not limited by income, veteran status, or whether the property is located in a rural area. However, the availability or attractiveness of FHA-insured mortgages may be limited by other factors, such as the maximum mortgage amount that FHA will insure, the fees that it charges for insurance, and its underwriting criteria.[3]

---

[1] Reverse mortgages allow elderly homeowners to access the equity in their homes as a source of income. The lender makes payments to the borrower, and is repaid with the proceeds from the sale of the home when the homeowner dies or chooses to no longer occupy the property. For more information on FHA-insured reverse mortgages, see CRS Report RL33843, *Reverse Mortgages: Background and Issues*, by Bruce E. Foote.

[2] VA provides guarantees on certain home mortgages made to veterans, and USDA insures certain home mortgages made to lower-income households in rural areas. For more information on VA- and USDA-guaranteed mortgages, see CRS Report R42504, *VA Housing: Guaranteed Loans, Direct Loans, and Specially Adapted Housing Grants*, by Libby Perl; and CRS Report RL31837, *An Overview of USDA Rural Development Programs*, by Tadlock Cowan.

[3] For more information on the specific features and requirements of FHA-insured loans, see CRS Report RS20530, *FHA-Insured Home Loans: An Overview*, by Katie Jones.

Background on FHA-Insured Mortgages

FHA insures mortgages made by private lenders against the possibility that the borrower will default on the mortgage. If the borrower does default on his or her mortgage and the loan goes to foreclosure, the lender submits an insurance claim to FHA. FHA pays the lender the amount still owed on the mortgage, and the lender conveys the foreclosed property to FHA to sell. To be eligible for FHA insurance, borrowers and mortgages must meet certain criteria, and lenders must be approved by FHA. FHA charges borrowers upfront and annual fees, known as mortgage insurance premiums, for the insurance. Historically, claims on FHA-insured mortgages have been paid for by these mortgage insurance premiums.

FHA-insured loans are generally obtained by homebuyers who might find it difficult, or more expensive, to obtain a mortgage in the absence of insurance. FHA-insured mortgages have lower downpayment requirements than most conventional mortgages. (Conventional mortgages are mortgages that are not insured by FHA or guaranteed by another government agency, such as VA or USDA.)[4] FHA will insure mortgages with downpayments as low as 3.5%. Because saving for a downpayment is often the biggest barrier to homeownership for first-time homebuyers and lower- or moderate-income borrowers, the smaller downpayment requirement for FHA-insured loans may allow these types of households to obtain a mortgage earlier than they otherwise could. Likewise, FHA-insured mortgages also have less stringent requirements related to credit history than many conventional loans. This might make FHA-insured mortgages attractive to borrowers without credit histories or with weaker credit histories, who would either find it difficult to take out a mortgage absent FHA insurance, or may find it more expensive to do so.[5]

Mortgages with smaller downpayments or made to borrowers with weaker credit histories are generally considered riskier than mortgages made to borrowers with higher downpayments and stronger credit histories. Therefore, in the absence of some kind of insurance, lenders might be unwilling to offer mortgages to these borrowers, or would charge higher interest rates to compensate for the increased risk that might be more than many of these borrowers could afford. This has led to a concern that some qualified borrowers who can sustain monthly mortgage payments might be unable to obtain affordable mortgages in the absence of mortgage insurance. By insuring the lender against the possibility of borrower default, mortgage insurance is intended to make lenders more willing to offer affordable mortgages to these borrowers.

In addition to government agencies such as FHA, private companies also offer mortgage insurance, known as private mortgage insurance (PMI). Conventional mortgages with downpayments of less than 20% are generally required to carry PMI.[6] FHA insurance, therefore, can act as an alternative to private mortgage insurance.[7]

---

[4] Conventional mortgages can include mortgages that are purchased by the government-sponsored enterprises (GSEs) Fannie Mae and Freddie Mac. Although technically not government agencies, Fannie Mae and Freddie Mac are currently under government conservatorship and are receiving government financial assistance. Mortgages that meet Fannie Mae's and Freddie Mac's criteria are referred to as conforming mortgages.

[5] Historically, many FHA-insured mortgages are made to borrowers with credit scores on the lower end of the spectrum. However, given the tightening of mortgage credit in response to the economic downturn in recent years, FHA has recently been insuring a greater share of mortgages to borrowers with higher credit scores. This is discussed in more detail in the "Changes to Downpayment and Credit Score Requirements" section later in this report.

[6] One reason for this is the requirements of Fannie Mae and Freddie Mac, which influence a large part of the mortgage market. By statute, Fannie Mae and Freddie Mac cannot purchase mortgages where the mortgage amount exceeds 80% of the value of the home unless the mortgage includes some kind of credit enhancement, such as private mortgage (continued...)

There are some differences between PMI and FHA insurance. For one thing, FHA insures the entire principal amount of the mortgage, while private mortgage insurance generally covers the amount of the mortgage that exceeds an 80% loan-to-value ratio (LTV).[8] Furthermore, PMI companies generally use a different fee structure than FHA, and often charge borrowers fees that vary based on features of the mortgage such as the loan-to-value ratio. FHA charges most borrowers the same fees regardless of credit score or loan-to-value ratio, except that there is a slight difference in the annual premium charged to loans with LTVs above or below 95%.[9] Whether PMI or FHA insurance is a more attractive option for a specific borrower will depend on a number of factors, including the respective underwriting standards and the fees charged by PMI companies and FHA at a given point in time and the specifics of the mortgage in question. In addition, private mortgage insurance companies are more likely to tighten their standards or reduce the number of loans they insure during economic downturns, but FHA insurance generally remains available to qualified borrowers regardless of market conditions.

There is no income limit to qualify for an FHA-insured mortgage. There is also not a specific minimum income requirement, although FHA borrowers must be fully underwritten in accordance with FHA criteria to ensure that they are an acceptable credit risk and have sufficient income or assets to repay a mortgage.[10] There is also a maximum mortgage amount that FHA will insure, which is set in statute and varies by area, with a national ceiling that cannot be exceeded.[11] Although borrowers of any income are eligible for FHA-insured mortgages, there are several reasons that wealthier borrowers or those who can afford larger downpayments would probably not choose an FHA-insured mortgage in most circumstances. For example, borrowers who can afford a downpayment of at least 20% can generally obtain a conventional loan without mortgage insurance of any kind. Furthermore, wealthier individuals are more likely to buy more expensive homes, and the maximum mortgage amount that FHA will insure might not be enough to purchase such homes.

Since FHA-insured mortgages are often obtained by borrowers who cannot make large downpayments or those with weaker credit histories, some have questioned whether FHA-insured

---

(...continued)

insurance.

[7] Borrowers with less than a 20% downpayment can have options other than mortgage insurance. For example, during the mid-2000s, it became more common for borrowers to take out a "piggyback loan," or a second mortgage to cover part or all of the purchase price that exceeded 80% of the value of the home. These types of loans became much less common as mortgage credit standards tightened in response to economic and housing market turmoil in the late 2000s.

[8] The loan-to-value ratio, or LTV, is the amount borrowed expressed as a percentage of the value of the home. For example, if someone puts down a 20% downpayment and takes out a mortgage for 80% of the home's purchase price, the LTV is 80%.

[9] In 2008, FHA announced that it planned to start charging mortgage insurance premiums that would vary based on loan-to-value ratios and credit scores. Congress imposed a one-year moratorium on this pricing structure in the Housing and Economic Recovery Act of 2008 (P.L. 110-289). FHA has not announced plans to move forward with such a pricing structure since the expiration of the moratorium. For more information, see FHA Mortgagee Letters 08-16 and 08-22 at http://portal.hud.gov/hudportal/HUD?src=/program_offices/administration/hudclips/letters/mortgagee/2008ml.

[10] FHA's underwriting criteria can be found in FHA Handbook 4155.1, "Mortgage Credit Analysis for Mortgage Insurance on One- to Four-Unit Mortgage Loans," available at http://portal.hud.gov/hudportal/HUD?src=/program_offices/administration/hudclips/handbooks/hsgh/4155.1.

[11] For more information on the maximum loan amounts that FHA insures, see CRS Report RS20530, *FHA-Insured Home Loans: An Overview*, by Katie Jones. For a discussion of recent debate about whether the loan limits should be allowed to decline in some areas, see CRS Report R42145, *Housing Issues in the 112th Congress*, coordinated by Katie Jones.

---

mortgages are similar to subprime mortgages.[12] FHA-insured mortgages and subprime mortgages may appeal to some of the same pool of borrowers. However, FHA-insured mortgages are prohibited from carrying the full range of features that many subprime mortgages could carry. For example, FHA-insured loans must be fully documented, and they cannot include features such as negative amortization.[13] (FHA mortgages can include adjustable interest rates.) Nevertheless, the types of mortgages that FHA insures are generally perceived to be riskier for lenders relative to conventional prime mortgages since downpayments are generally lower and borrowers are more likely to have weaker credit histories.

FHA's Market Share

Traditionally, FHA plays a countercyclical role in the mortgage market, meaning that it tends to insure more mortgages when mortgage credit markets are tight and fewer mortgages when mortgage credit is more widely available. A major reason for this is that FHA continues to insure mortgages that meet its standards even during market downturns or in regions experiencing economic turmoil. When the economy is weak and lenders and private mortgage insurers might tighten credit standards and reduce lending activity, FHA-insured mortgages may be the only mortgages available to some borrowers, or may have more favorable terms than mortgages that lenders are willing to make without FHA insurance. When the economy is strong and mortgage credit is more widely available, many borrowers may find it easier to qualify for conventional mortgages.

FHA's market share can be measured in a number of different ways. It can be computed as the *number* of FHA-insured mortgages originated divided by the total number of mortgages originated, or as the *dollar volume* of FHA-insured mortgages originated divided by the total dollar volume of mortgages originated. Furthermore, FHA's market share is sometimes reported as a share of *all mortgages*, and sometimes only as a share of *home purchase mortgages* (as opposed to both purchase mortgages and refinance mortgages). Finally, a market share figure can be reported as a share of all mortgages *originated within a specific time period*, such as a given year, or as a share of all mortgages *outstanding at a point in time*, regardless of when they were originated. When considering FHA's market share, it is important to recognize which of these figures is being reported.

Figure 1 shows FHA's market share between 2001 and 2011, as a percentage of the number of all newly originated mortgages, newly originated purchase mortgages only, and newly originated refinance mortgages only in each year. FHA's share of home purchase mortgages tends to be the highest, largely because borrowers who refinance are more likely to have built up a greater amount of equity in their homes and, therefore, might refinance out of FHA-insured mortgages into conventional mortgages.

---

[12] There is not a consensus definition of subprime mortgages, but they generally refer to mortgages made to borrowers with credit scores below a certain threshold. Many subprime mortgages contained non-traditional features, but not all subprime mortgages contained these features, and a mortgage does not have to have non-traditional features to be considered subprime. For more information on how FHA-insured mortgages compare to subprime mortgages, see CRS Report R40937, *The Federal Housing Administration (FHA) and Risky Lending*, by Darryl E. Getter.

[13] With a negative amortization loan, borrowers have the option to pay less than the full amount of the interest due for a set period of time. The loan "negatively amortizes" as the remaining interest is added to the outstanding loan balance, so that the loan balance increases over the time rather than decreasing as it would with positive amortization.

Figure 1. FHA Share of the Mortgage Market, 2001-2011

% of total mortgages originated in each year

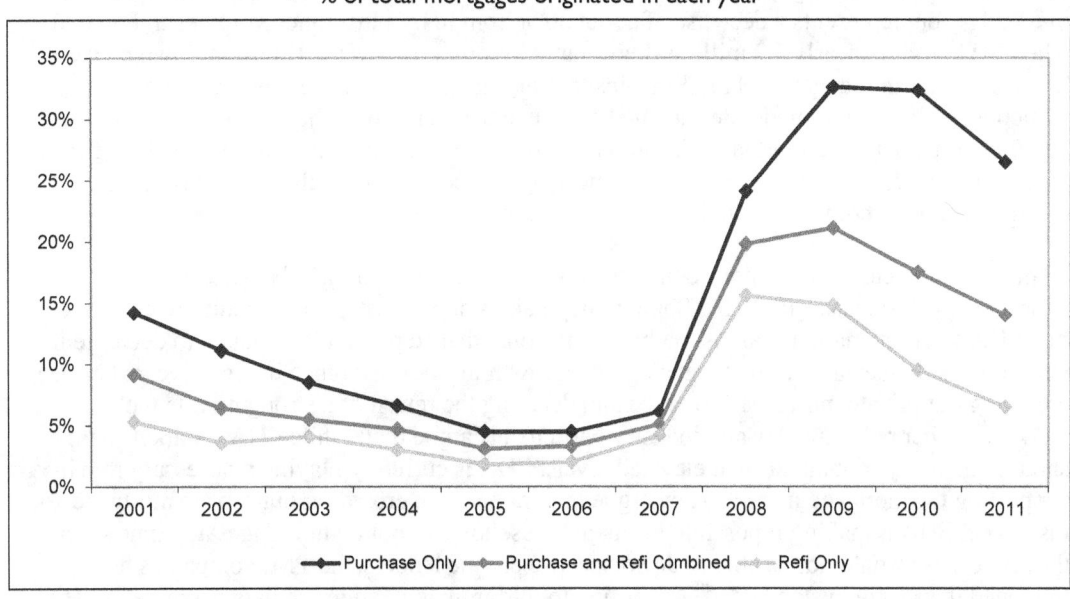

Source: Figure created by CRS based on data from *U.S. Department of Housing and Urban Development, FHA-Insured Single-Family Mortgage Market Share Report, 2012 – Quarter 2*, p. 2, http://portal.hud.gov/hudportal/documents/huddoc?id=fhamktq2_2012.pdf.

In the early 2000s, FHA-insured mortgages generally made up between 10% and 15% of the home-purchase mortgage market, as measured by number of mortgages. However, by 2005, FHA's market share had fallen to less than 5% of home-purchase mortgages. Subsequently, as economic conditions worsened and mortgage credit tightened, FHA's market share rose sharply, peaking at over 30% of home-purchase mortgages in 2009 and 2010, and over 20% of all mortgages (including both home purchases and refinances) in 2010. In 2011, FHA's market share fell slightly, but was still over 26% for home-purchase mortgages and nearly 15% for all mortgages.

The increase in FHA's market share since 2007 is due to a variety of factors related to housing market turmoil and broader economic instability. One factor is that economic conditions led many banks to limit their lending activities, including lending for mortgages. Similarly, private mortgage insurance companies, facing steep losses from past mortgages, began tightening the underwriting criteria for mortgages that they would insure.[14] Another factor is an increase in the maximum mortgage amounts that FHA can insure, enacted by Congress in 2008, which may have made FHA-insured mortgages a more viable option for some borrowers in areas where FHA had been previously "priced out" of the market.[15]

---

[14] For example, see Avery, Robert B., Neil Bhutta, Kenneth P. Brevoort, and Glenn B. Canner, *The 2009 HMDA Data: The Mortgage Market in a Time of Low Interest Rates and Economic Distress*, http://www.federalreserve.gov/pubs/bulletin/2010/articles/2009HMDA/default.htm. See also Radian's 2010 annual report, at http://www.radian.biz/sfc/servlet.shepherd/version/download/068C0000000SKI1IAO. Page 79 includes a discussion of Radian, a private mortgage insurer, tightening its underwriting standards.

[15] By statute, FHA can only insure mortgages up to a certain principal amount. For more information on the current and recent maximum loan amounts that FHA can insure, see CRS Report RS20530, *FHA-Insured Home Loans: An Overview*, by Katie Jones. The maximum mortgage amounts that FHA can insure in high-cost areas are scheduled to (continued...)

FHA insured nearly 1.2 million single-family mortgages in FY2012, nearly 734,000 (about 62%) of which were for home purchases. This was similar to the number of mortgages insured by FHA in FY2011, but represents a decrease of about 30% from FHA's insurance volumes in FY2010, when FHA insured nearly 1.7 million single-family mortgages, over 1.1 million of which were home purchase mortgages.[16] Many FHA-insured mortgages are obtained by first-time homebuyers, lower-and moderate-income homebuyers, and minority homebuyers. Of the over 700,000 home purchase mortgages insured by FHA in FY2012, about 78% were made to first-time homebuyers.[17] In 2011, FHA-insured mortgages accounted for half of home purchase mortgages among both black and Hispanic borrowers.[18]

While not the focus of this report, policymakers have had an ongoing debate about the appropriate market share for FHA. Some policymakers and industry participants are concerned that FHA's current market share is too high, and argue that steps should be taken to decrease its market share immediately. They argue that the growth in FHA insurance in recent years has been crowding out private mortgage insurance and delaying the return of a strong private mortgage market.[19] Other policymakers and industry participants argue that, while FHA's market share should not always remain at such elevated levels, FHA is currently playing a necessary role in supporting the mortgage market. They argue that, rather than crowding out private mortgage insurance, FHA is making it possible for many households to obtain mortgages at a time when they otherwise would not be able to do so because private lenders and PMI companies have tightened their lending standards.[20] According to this argument, an immediate decrease in FHA's market share could make it difficult for many households to obtain mortgages, which could in turn further destabilize housing markets by lowering demand and further depressing home prices. Policymakers are likely to continue to debate the appropriate market role for FHA, both in the short term as well as in the longer term. For example, FHA's role in the market might be considered as part of broader debate about the future of the U.S. housing finance system.

(...continued)

decrease from their current levels at the end of 2013.

[16] U.S. Department of Housing and Urban Development, *Annual Report to Congress on the Financial Status of the FHA Mutual Mortgage Insurance Fund, Fiscal Year 2012*, November 16, 2012, p. 12, http://portal.hud.gov/hudportal/documents/huddoc?id=F12MMIFundRepCong111612.pdf.

[17] Ibid., p. 7.

[18] Ibid., p. 20.

[19] For example, see U.S. Congress, House Committee on Financial Services, Subcommittee on Insurance, Housing and Community Opportunity, *Legislative Proposals to Determine the Future Role of FHA, RHS, and GNMA in the Single- and Multi-Family Mortgage Markets, Part 1*, 112th Congress, 1st. sess., May 25, 2011, H. Hrg. 112-32 (Washington: GPO, 2012), http://financialservices.house.gov/uploadedfiles/112-32.pdf, and *Legislative Proposals to Determine the Future Role of FHA, RHS, and GNMA in the Single- and Multi-Family Mortgage Markets, Part 2*, 112th Cong., 1st sess., September 8, 2011, H. Hrg. 112-57 (Washington: GPO, 2012), http://financialservices.house.gov/uploadedfiles/112-57.pdf.

[20] Ibid.

Financial Status of the Mutual Mortgage Insurance Fund

FHA-insured single-family mortgages are administered under an insurance fund known as the Mutual Mortgage Insurance Fund (MMI Fund). Money flows into the MMI Fund primarily from sources such as the mortgage insurance premiums paid by borrowers and sales of foreclosed properties, and money flows out of the MMI Fund primarily from claims paid to lenders when FHA-insured mortgages default. The MMI Fund is required to be self-supporting, meaning that it is supposed to pay for costs related to insured loans (such as insurance claims) with money it earns on those loans (such as through premiums), not through appropriations. It is also required to hold funds beyond what it needs to pay for expected losses on insured loans in reserve to cover any increases in expected losses. In recent years, increasing losses on FHA-insured loans have led to concern about the MMI Fund's financial status and whether it might exhaust these funds. If this occurred, the MMI Fund could require funds from the Department of the Treasury (Treasury) to hold in reserve against expected losses or, eventually, to pay insurance claims.

This section of the report focuses on certain concepts that are often discussed in relation to the MMI Fund's financial health. First, it provides a brief discussion of some of the major factors that affect the financial soundness of the MMI Fund, namely, default rates on FHA-insured loans, current economic conditions, and projections of future economic conditions. Second, it describes how the MMI Fund is treated in the federal budget process, which determines whether FHA will ever need an appropriation to insure new loans in an upcoming fiscal year or whether FHA will need funds from Treasury to pay for higher-than-expected losses on loans insured in past years. (Historically, FHA has never needed either an appropriation to insure new loans or funds from Treasury to pay claims.) Finally, it briefly describes measures of the MMI Fund's actuarial soundness that are reported in an annual independent actuarial review; this actuarial review is discussed in more detail in the **Appendix**.

Broadly speaking, the budgetary treatment and the actuarial soundness of the MMI Fund are two different ways of looking at the same thing—namely, how the loans insured under the MMI Fund have performed and are expected to perform in the future, and the effect of this loan performance on the financial position of the MMI Fund—and both are important for understanding the MMI Fund's financial status. One concept related to the actuarial review, the capital ratio, receives much attention and is an important indicator of the financial soundness of the MMI Fund that helps to illuminate the likelihood of FHA needing funds from Treasury. However, it is concepts related to the budgetary treatment of FHA-insured loans, not the capital ratio, that actually determine whether or not the MMI Fund will require any assistance from Treasury. This will be described in more detail later in this section.

Default Rates on FHA-Insured Loans

When an FHA-insured mortgage defaults, FHA pays a claim to the lender for the remaining amount that the borrower owes on the mortgage. The loss to FHA is the claim amount paid plus any other foreclosure-related expenses, minus any amount that FHA can recoup by selling the foreclosed home. FHA's total losses related to defaults and foreclosures can depend on, among other factors, the number of delinquencies, defaults, and foreclosures on FHA-insured loans; the success of efforts to help borrowers avoid foreclosure on FHA-insured loans or to minimize the costs to FHA associated with a foreclosure on an FHA-insured loan; and how much FHA can recoup by reselling foreclosed homes.

Like default and foreclosure rates on other types of mortgages, default and foreclosure rates on FHA-insured mortgages have been elevated in recent years. This rise in default rates has led to an increase in FHA's actual losses, as well as an increase in the losses that it expects to incur in the future related to loans that it currently insures. This has put pressure on the MMI Fund. As of October 2012, FHA reported that over 734,000 out of 7.7 million insured single-family mortgages (about 9.5%) were seriously delinquent, meaning that they were 90 days or more past due, in the foreclosure process, or in bankruptcy.[21]

Figure 2 shows the rate of FHA-insured mortgages that were seriously delinquent in recent years compared to prime mortgages, subprime mortgages, and all mortgages. FHA-insured loans have performed better than subprime loans, but not as well as prime loans. Generally speaking, FHA-insured loans are expected to have somewhat higher default rates than prime loans, since FHA-insured loans generally go to borrowers who have smaller downpayments or weaker credit histories than borrowers with prime conventional loans. While the serious delinquency rate on FHA-insured loans has increased, it has not experienced the same sharp increase in delinquency rates that subprime loans have experienced in recent years. The subprime delinquency rate was nearly 23% in the second quarter of 2012.

---

[21] Federal Housing Administration, Office of Risk Analysis and Regulatory Affairs, *Monthly Report to the FHA Commissioner on FHA Business Activity*, October 2012, p. 12, http://portal.hud.gov/hudportal/documents/huddoc?id= 12oct.pdf.

Figure 2. Serious Delinquency Rates

QI 2006-Q2 2012

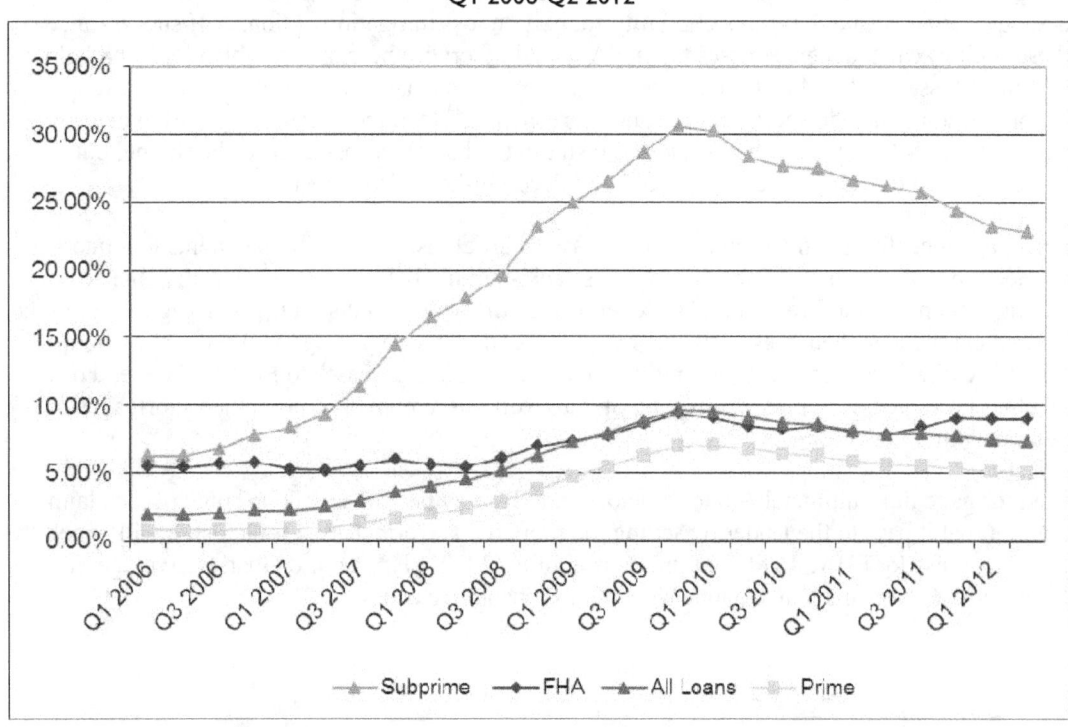

Source: Figure created by CRS based on data from the Mortgage Bankers Association.

A number of factors are contributing to the increase in default rates on FHA-insured mortgages. Unfavorable economic conditions, such as decreases in home prices and increases in unemployment, have continued to affect many regions of the country, leading to more defaults and foreclosures on FHA-insured loans. Other factors, such as the credit quality of some loans, have also contributed to increased default rates. The loans that were originated between FY2005 and FY2008 appear to be performing especially poorly. (See **Table 1** later in this report, which shows that the loans insured in these years are now expected to lose between .05 cents and .09 cents per dollar of loans insured.) One reason for this is that these mortgages were originated at the height of the housing bubble, and therefore were most affected by factors such as subsequent home price declines.[22] Loans insured over this time period were also of a lower credit quality, on average, than loans insured more recently, partly because borrowers with stronger credit histories could more easily find cheaper mortgages that were not insured by FHA. Another reason is that the loans insured in these years have a higher concentration of mortgages that benefitted from a practice known as seller-funded downpayment assistance, and these loans have had especially high default rates. FHA is no longer permitted to insure loans with this type of downpayment assistance. (For more information on seller-funded downpayment assistance and the performance of these loans, see the "Prohibition on Seller-Funded Downpayment Assistance" subsection in the "Selected Recent FHA Policy Changes" section of this report.)

---

[22] U.S. Department of Housing and Urban Development, *Annual Report to Congress on the Financial Status of the FHA Mutual Mortgage Insurance Fund, Fiscal Year 2011*, November 15, 2011, p. 42, http://portal.hud.gov/hudportal/documents/huddoc?id=fhammifannrptfy2011.pdf.

Efforts to help borrowers avoid foreclosure, such as loan modifications, are known as loss mitigation actions. When a borrower with an FHA-insured loan defaults, the servicer of the loan is required to evaluate the loan's eligibility for certain loss mitigation options.[23] If successful, these options can reduce the losses that FHA would otherwise bear on a troubled loan and help minimize losses to the MMI Fund. Loss mitigation options that can result in a borrower keeping his or her home include special forbearance agreements,[24] loan modifications,[25] partial claims,[26] and FHA-HAMP.[27] Other options that will result in the borrower losing his or her home, but avoiding foreclosure, include short sales[28] and deeds-in-lieu of foreclosure.[29]

FHA pays incentive payments and, in some cases, partial insurance claim payments to lenders in connection with loss mitigation actions. These costs are likely to be less to FHA than the cost of paying a claim after a foreclosure. However, if the borrower defaults on the mortgage again in the future, and the loan then goes to foreclosure, FHA could end up paying the full claim amount. Therefore, the extent to which loss mitigation actions minimize losses to FHA will depend on whether borrowers who receive any type of loan workout remain current on their mortgages or default again in the future.

If a mortgage must ultimately go to foreclosure, FHA may be able to recoup some of the claim amount that it pays to the lender by selling the property. Nevertheless, a foreclosure will generally result in a loss for FHA. As of the third quarter of FY2012, FHA reported that, on average, it loses about 63% of the loan balance when it pays insurance claims.[30]

---

[23] See Federal Housing Administration, FHA Mortgagee Letter 00-05, "Loss Mitigation Program – Comprehensive Clarification of Policy and Notice of Procedural Changes," available at http://portal.hud.gov/hudportal/HUD?src=/ program_offices/administration/hudclips/letters/mortgagee/2000ml, as well as subsequent Mortgagee Letters.

[24] Forbearance agreements allow a borrower to make lower mortgage payments for a specified period of time, and to repay the difference between the lower mortgage payment and the actual amount owed at a later date. For more information on FHA's forbearance options, see http://portal.hud.gov/hudportal/documents/huddoc?id=nscsffaq.pdf.

[25] Loan modifications change one or more of the features of the mortgage, such as the interest rate or the term of the mortgage, to lower a borrower's monthly mortgage payments. For more information on FHA's loan modification options, see http://portal.hud.gov/hudportal/documents/huddoc?id=nsclmfaq.pdf.

[26] Partial claims allow a borrower to become current again on a delinquent mortgage through an advance of funds from the lender on the borrower's behalf to reinstate the mortgage. FHA pays the lender for this advance of funds—called a partial claim, because the amount paid by FHA is only part of what the full claim amount would be if the loan went through foreclosure—and the borrower repays FHA in the future. For more information on FHA's partial claim option, see http://portal.hud.gov/hudportal/documents/huddoc?id=nscpcfaq.pdf.

[27] FHA-HAMP essentially combines a loan modification and a partial claim amount to modify a borrower's loan to achieve an affordable payment. The option was created to parallel the broader Home Affordable Modification Program (HAMP), but it differs in some important ways from HAMP. For more information on FHA-HAMP, see http://portal.hud.gov/hudportal/documents/huddoc?id=nschampfact.pdf. For more information on regular HAMP, see CRS Report R40210, *Preserving Homeownership: Foreclosure Prevention Initiatives*, by Katie Jones.

[28] Short sales allow a borrower to sell the home for less than the full amount owed on the mortgage, and the lender accepts the proceeds of the sale as payment in full. For more information on FHA's short sale options, see http://portal.hud.gov/hudportal/documents/huddoc?id=nscpfsfaq.pdf.

[29] A deed-in-lieu of foreclosure allows the borrower to surrender the deed to the property as payment in full on the mortgage. For more information on FHA's deed-in-lieu of foreclosure options, see http://portal.hud.gov/hudportal/ documents/huddoc?id=nscdilfaq.pdf.

[30] U.S. Department of Housing and Urban Development, *Quarterly Report to Congress on the Status of the MMI Fund, Q3 2012*, p. 8, available at http://portal.hud.gov/hudportal/HUD?src=/program_offices/housing/rmra/oe/rpts/rtc/ fhartcqtrly.

The Role of Economic Conditions, Projections, and Assumptions

Economic and housing market conditions impact FHA's financial position in a few different ways. First of all, economic conditions can contribute to default and foreclosure rates. If more people are unemployed or underemployed, or if home prices fall such that people cannot sell their homes if they can no longer afford their mortgages, then more people may face default or foreclosure. Falling house prices also limit the amount that FHA can recoup when it sells a foreclosed property.

Projections of future economic conditions are also important factors in evaluating the health of the MMI Fund. The future path of house prices and interest rates, in particular, play large roles in estimating how FHA-insured mortgages will perform in the future and, ultimately, how much money is expected to flow into and out of the MMI Fund. The future path of house prices is important because, as noted, house prices play a role in default and foreclosure rates and in how much FHA can recoup on foreclosures. Interest rates are important because they can affect home purchase activity as well as the decision by homeowners to refinance their mortgages, which affects how much premium revenue FHA expects to bring in and its potential liability for future claims.

Estimates of the MMI Fund's current financial health rely on assumptions about how loans that are currently insured by FHA will perform in the future. Estimates of the MMI Fund's future financial health also rely on assumptions about how these loans that FHA currently insures will perform in the future, but, in addition, they rely upon assumptions about how many new loans FHA is likely to insure in future years and how those future loans will perform. If assumptions about future economic conditions or FHA's future business are not accurate—for example, if FHA insures more or fewer loans than anticipated in the future, or if current and future loans perform better or worse than expected—then estimates of FHA's current or future financial positions may also not be accurate.

The MMI Fund in the Federal Budget

This section describes how FHA-insured mortgages are accounted for in the federal budget in the year that the loans are insured and in the years thereafter. It includes a discussion of the circumstances under which the MMI Fund would need an appropriation to insure new loans in an upcoming fiscal year, and the circumstances under which the MMI Fund can draw on permanent and indefinite budget authority with Treasury to reserve for higher-than-expected losses on loans insured in past years.

Credit Reform Accounting and Credit Subsidy Rates

The Federal Credit Reform Act of 1990 (FCRA) specifies the way in which the costs of federal loan guarantees, including FHA-insured loans, are recorded in the federal budget.[31] The FCRA requires that, like all federal loan guarantees, the amount of money that FHA-insured loans are projected to cost the government or earn for the government over the life of those loans be

---

[31] For more information on how the costs of federal credit programs are treated in the federal budget, see CRS Report R42632, *Budgetary Treatment of Federal Credit (Direct Loans and Loan Guarantees): Concepts, History, and Issues for the 112th Congress*, by James M. Bickley.

recorded in the federal budget in the year that the loans are insured.[32] In accordance with the FCRA, the amount that FHA expects to eventually earn or lose for every dollar of mortgages that it will insure in the upcoming fiscal year is estimated and reflected in the federal budget as a *credit subsidy rate*.[33]

Since credit reform accounting was implemented, the single-family mortgages that FHA has expected to insure in a given year have always been estimated to have a negative credit subsidy rate in that year's budget.[34] A negative credit subsidy rate indicates that, in present value terms, more money is expected to come into the insurance fund than is expected to flow out of the insurance fund in relation to loans insured in a given year. In other words, a negative subsidy rate means that, over the life of the loans, the insured loans are projected to make money for the government rather than require an appropriation from the government in order to operate. (This applies only to the costs associated with the insured loans themselves; credit subsidy rates do not include the administrative costs of a program. FHA does receive an appropriation for administrative contract expenses and for salaries.)[35] When a loan guarantee program has a negative credit subsidy rate, it results in *offsetting receipts*. In the case of the MMI Fund, these offsetting receipts can offset other costs of the HUD budget.[36]

Each year, FHA and the Office of Management and Budget (OMB) estimate the credit subsidy rate for the loans expected to be insured in the upcoming fiscal year in the President's budget request.[37] These estimates are based on factors such as projections of how much mortgage insurance premium revenue the loans insured in the upcoming year are expected to bring in, projections of how much FHA will have to pay in future insurance claims related to those loans, and projections of how much money FHA will be able to recover by selling foreclosed properties. These projections, in turn, rest on assumptions about the credit quality of the loans being made and assumptions about future economic conditions (including house prices and interest rates).

---

[32] For more detailed information on how loan guarantees are recorded in the federal budget under the Federal Credit Reform Act, see CRS Report R42632, *Budgetary Treatment of Federal Credit (Direct Loans and Loan Guarantees): Concepts, History, and Issues for the 112th Congress*, by James M. Bickley.

[33] In technical terms, a credit subsidy rate is calculated as the net present value of expected future cash flows from mortgages insured in a given year, divided by the dollar volume of loans expected to be insured in that year. The "net present value of expected future cash flows" is the present value of expected cash flows out of the insurance fund (such as claims expected to be paid in the future on defaulted mortgages) net of expected cash flows into the insurance fund (such as premiums expected to be paid by borrowers).

[34] While FHA's traditional single-family mortgage program has always been estimated to have a negative credit subsidy rate in the year that the loans are insured, other FHA programs have at times been estimated to have positive credit subsidy rates.

[35] In FY2012, FHA received an appropriation of $207 million for administrative contract expenses for all of its programs, including multifamily and healthcare facilities programs. The President's FY2013 budget requests $215 million for administrative contract expenses. Funding for salaries is appropriated as part of HUD's overall appropriation for salaries and expenses. Annual appropriations laws also include a maximum dollar volume of loans that FHA can insure in a given fiscal year. In FY2012, the maximum dollar volume of loans that FHA could insure under the MMI Fund was $400 billion.

[36] For more information on recent trends in FHA offsetting receipts and their role in the budget process, see CRS Report R42542, *Department of Housing and Urban Development (HUD): Funding Trends Since FY2002*, by Maggie McCarty.

[37] FHA, in conjunction with the Office of Management and Budget (OMB), estimates the expected gain or cost of insuring mortgages in the next fiscal year in the President's annual budget requests. The Congressional Budget Office (CBO) re-estimates these expected gains or costs using its own models and assumptions. The CBO re-estimated numbers are the ones that matter for the purposes of federal budgeting and appropriations.

Since the Federal Credit Reform Act went into effect, the original credit subsidy rate estimates for FHA-insured loans have ranged from a low of -0.05% in FY2009, meaning that FHA originally expected to earn .0005 cents for every dollar of loans it insured in that year, to a high of -3.10% in FY2011, meaning that FHA originally expected to make .0310 cents for every dollar of loans insured in that year.[38] (The total amount of money that FHA would expect to make on loans insured in a given year would also depend on the total dollar amount of loans it expected to insure in that year.) In all cases, the loans expected to be insured by FHA in a given year have been projected to make money.

If FHA's single-family program was ever estimated to have a positive credit subsidy rate for the upcoming fiscal year, it would require an appropriation from Congress to cover the difference between the amount of money FHA expected to take in and pay out over the life of the loans.[39] If Congress did not appropriate funding to cover a positive subsidy rate, then FHA would not be able to insure new loans in that year. (For a brief discussion of a proposed change in the required method of calculating credit subsidy rates that could result in the MMI Fund having a positive credit subsidy rate, see the nearby text box, "FHA and "Fair Value" Accounting.")

FHA and "Fair Value" Accounting

FHA's credit subsidy rates are calculated in accordance with the methodology specified in the FCRA. This methodology takes into account expected costs (primarily claims) and gains (primarily premium revenue) associated with loans insured in a given year, and arrives at a net present value of the future cash flows on these loans by using interest rates on Treasury bonds as a discount rate. The interest rate on Treasury bonds does not account for market risk, because Treasury bonds are assumed to be virtually risk-free. However, some have suggested that credit subsidy rate estimates would more accurately reflect actual loan performance if the discount rate included adjustments for market risk. Accounting for market risk in calculating credit subsidy is referred to as the "fair value" approach.

The Congressional Budget Office (CBO) has released a report that discusses the difference between FCRA accounting and a fair value approach specifically as it relates to FHA. (See Congressional Budget Office, *Accounting for FHA's Single-Family Mortgage Insurance Program on a Fair-Value Basis*, May 18, 2011, http://www.cbo.gov/publication/41445.) The CBO report finds that using a fair value approach would have changed the estimate of FY2012 credit subsidy for the MMI Fund programs from a negative number to a positive number. This means that, had the fair value approach been used, the loans that FHA expected to insure in that year would have been projected to lose money rather than earn money over the life of the loans, and FHA would have required an appropriation from Congress in order to insure loans in that year.

The debate over how to calculate subsidy rates for FHA's loan program is part of a larger debate over whether subsidy costs of government loan guarantees in general should reflect an adjustment for market risk. In the 112th Congress, a bill requiring fair value accounting for federal credit programs passed the House (H.R. 3581). For more information on the issues involved, see CRS Report R42503, *Subsidy Cost of Federal Credit: Cost to the Government or Fair Value Cost?*, by James M. Bickley.

In its FY2013 Budget Justifications, FHA estimated that the credit subsidy rate for the MMI Fund, excluding reverse mortgages, would be -5.38%. This means that for every dollar of single-family loans that it insures in FY2013, FHA expects to earn $0.0538 for the government. Since FHA is projecting that it will insure $149 billion in single-family mortgages in FY2013, FHA expects the mortgages

---

[38] Some examples of reasons for the differences in the original credit subsidy rates across years could include differences in the mortgage insurance premiums that were being charged in that year, differences in the anticipated credit quality of loans being insured, or differences in the expected future trajectory of economic factors (such as interest rates or house prices) that can impact prepayments, defaults, and the amount that FHA can recover after a foreclosure.

[39] The Congressional Budget Office (CBO) does its own estimate of the subsidy rate, using its own assumptions and models. CBO's estimate of the subsidy rate is the one that matters for the purposes of the appropriations process, including determining whether the FHA single-family mortgage insurance program will require an appropriation and for determining the amount of any receipts available to offset the cost of the HUD budget.

it insures in FY2013 to generate about $8 billion in negative credit subsidy.[40] When FHA-insured reverse mortgages are included, FHA expects the loans insured under the MMI Fund to generate a total of about $8.2 billion in negative credit subsidy.[41]

Credit Subsidy Rate Re-estimates

The amount of money that loans insured by FHA in a given year actually earn for or cost the government over the course of their life is likely to be different from the original credit subsidy estimates due to better or worse than expected performance of those loans. Federal credit reform accounting recognizes this, and provides permanent and indefinite budget authority to federal credit programs to cover any increased costs of loan guarantees.

Each year, in consultation with OMB, FHA re-estimates each prior year's credit subsidy rates based on the actual performance of the loans and other factors, such as updated economic projections. Although the original credit subsidy rate for the single-family mortgage insurance program each year has historically been negative, in recent years, the credit subsidy rate re-estimates for several cohorts of loans have been estimated to be positive, suggesting that FHA will actually lose money on the loans insured in those years. Even if this is the case, FHA will not necessarily need to draw on its permanent and indefinite budget authority with Treasury to cover these losses if the amount it makes on loans insured in other years is enough to cover the difference. However, if the amount that FHA earns on loans insured in other years is not enough to cover these losses, it could need to draw on its permanent and indefinite budget authority with Treasury.

Table 1 shows the original credit subsidy rate estimates and the most current re-estimated credit subsidy rates for the loans insured in each fiscal year between 1992 and 2011. The first column shows the original credit subsidy rate. In all cases, the original subsidy rate estimates were negative (shown in green), meaning that the loans insured in those years were originally expected to make money for the government. The second column shows the current re-estimated credit subsidy rate for each year. Re-estimated credit subsidy rates are shown in green if they remained negative (even if they are less favorable than the original estimate) and in red if they have become positive.

For most years, the current re-estimated credit subsidy rate is less favorable than the original estimate, although many of the re-estimated credit subsidy rates are still negative. A lower, but still negative, credit subsidy estimate suggests that a particular cohort of loans will still make money for the government, but less than was originally estimated. In some years, particularly between FY2002 and FY2009, the re-estimates of the subsidy rates are positive (shown in red), meaning that these cohorts of loans are currently expected to lose money overall. In a few cases, namely, FY1992, FY2010, and FY2011, the current re-estimated subsidy rate is more favorable

---

[40] U.S. Department of Housing and Urban Development, *FY2012 Congressional Budget Justifications*, p. B-9, http://portal.hud.gov/hudportal/documents/huddoc?id=CombinedFHAFund.pdf.

[41] According to Senate Appropriations Committee documents, CBO estimates that FHA's MMI Fund, including reverse mortgages, will generate nearly $9.7 billion in negative credit subsidy in FY2013, a higher amount than HUD's estimate. See U.S. Congress, Senate Committee on Appropriations, *Transportation and Housing and Urban Development, and Related Agencies Appropriations Bill, 2013*, report to accompany S. 2322, 112th Cong., 2nd sess., April 19, 2012, S.Rept. 112-157 (Washington: GPO, 2012), p. 166, http://www.gpo.gov/fdsys/pkg/CRPT-112srpt157/pdf/CRPT-112srpt157.pdf.

than the original estimated subsidy rate, meaning that the loans insured in those years are now expected to make more money than originally estimated.

Table 1. MMI Fund Credit Subsidy Rates and Re-estimates

FY1992-FY2011

Fiscal Year	Original Subsidy Rate	Re-estimated Subsidy Rate
1992	-2.60	-3.22
1993	-2.70	-2.67
1994	-2.79	-1.81
1995	-1.95	-0.76
1996	-2.77	-1.08
1997	-2.88	-1.05
1998	-2.99	-1.49
1999	-2.62	-1.33
2000	-1.99	0.16
2001	-2.15	-0.08
2002	-2.07	0.31
2003	-2.53	1.29
2004	-2.47	1.80
2005	-1.80	5.21
2006	-1.70	6.42
2007	-0.37	9.28
2008	-0.25	6.36
2009	-0.05	1.07
2010	-0.86	-1.28
2011	-3.10	-4.53

Source: Table created by CRS based on Office of Management and Budget, *The President's Budget for Fiscal Year 2013, Federal Credit Supplement Spreadsheets, Loan Guarantees: Subsidy Reestimates,* http://www.whitehouse.gov/omb/budget/Supplemental/.

Notes: Negative credit subsidy re-estimates are in green; positive credit subsidy re-estimates are in red.

The MMI Fund Account Balances

The credit subsidy rate re-estimates affect the way in which funds are held in the MMI Fund. The MMI Fund consists of two primary accounts: the Financing Account and the Capital Reserve Account. The Financing Account holds funds to cover *expected* losses on FHA-insured loans. The Capital Reserve Account holds additional funds to cover *unexpected* losses. Funds are transferred between the two accounts each year on the basis of the re-estimated credit subsidy rates to ensure that enough is held in the Financing Account to cover updated projections of expected losses on insured loans. If the credit subsidy rate re-estimates reflect an aggregate increase in expected losses, then funds are transferred from the Capital Reserve Account to the Financing Account to cover the amount of the increase in expected losses. Conversely, if the credit subsidy rate re-estimates reflect a decrease in aggregate expected losses, then funds are transferred from the Financing Account to the Capital Reserve Account.

In recent years, the credit subsidy rate re-estimates have shown aggregate increases in expected losses on FHA-insured loans, requiring large transfers of funds from the Capital Reserve Account to the Financing Account to cover these additional expected future losses. **Table 2** illustrates the changes in these account balances between FY2008 and FY2012. At the end of FY2008, the MMI Fund held $19.3 billion in the Capital Reserve Account and $9 billion in the Financing Account. By the end of FY2012, FHA held $3.3 billion in the Capital Reserve Account and $27.1 billion in the Financing Account.[42]

Table 2. MMI Fund Account Balances, FY2008-FY2012

$ in billions

	Financing Account	Capital Reserve Account	Total
FY2008	$9.0	$19.3	$28.2
FY2009	$21.1	$10.7	$31.8
FY2010	$28.9	$4.4	$33.3
FY2011	$29.0	$4.7	$33.7
FY2012	$27.1	$3.3	$30.4

Source: FHA's FY2012 Annual Report to Congress on the Financial Status of the MMI Fund, page 31

Notes: Figures are as of the fourth quarter of each fiscal year.

While the amounts held in the Capital Reserve Account have been falling in recent years, the total amount that FHA has on hand (the combined amounts in the Financing Account and the Capital Reserve Account) has increased slightly since FY2008, to $30.4 billion in FY2012 from $28.2 billion in FY2008. However, since expected losses have also been increasing, more funds are currently held in the Financing Account to cover the increase in expected losses and less funds are held in the Capital Reserve Account. Although the total amount of resources on hand has been fairly steady in recent years, the cash flows from insurance operations (e.g., premiums paid in and claims paid out) have been negative, meaning that FHA has been paying out more money than it has been collecting. Insurance operations saw $2.8 billion of net cash outflow in FY2012, when FHA paid $18 billion in insurance claims.[43]

---

[42] U.S. Department of Housing and Urban Development, *Annual Report to Congress on the Financial Status of the FHA Mutual Mortgage Insurance Fund, FY2012*, November 16, 2012, p. 31. Information on the amounts held in the Financing Account and the Capital Reserve Account can also be found in FHA's Quarterly Reports to Congress on FHA Single-Family Mutual Mortgage Insurance Fund Programs, available at http://portal.hud.gov/hudportal/HUD?src=/program_offices/housing/rmra/oe/rpts/rtc/fhartcqtrly. These quarterly reports were required by Congress in the Housing and Economic Recovery Act of 2008 (P.L. 110-289).

[43] U.S. Department of Housing and Urban Development, *FHA Annual Report to Congress on the Financial Status of the MMI Fund, FY2012*, p. 32, http://portal.hud.gov/hudportal/documents/huddoc?id=F12MMIFundRepCong111612.pdf.

Although total resources have increased slightly since FY2008 (while the amount of reserves held in the Capital Reserve Account was decreasing), the total dollar volume of mortgages insured by FHA has also increased, from about $400 billion at the end of FY2008 to over $1.1 trillion at the end of FY2012.[44] Therefore, while capital resources held in the MMI Fund have increased by about $2 billion since FY2008, the amount of outstanding insurance-in-force has increased by more than $600 billion, meaning that FHA is holding about the same amount of total resources in the MMI Fund against a much higher dollar volume of insured mortgages.

Permanent and Indefinite Budget Authority

As noted, in light of the fact that estimating the cost of a loan guarantee program is inexact, the Federal Credit Reform Act of 1990 includes permanent and indefinite budget authority for federal loan guarantee programs to cover the cost of credit subsidy rate re-estimates. Therefore, if FHA ever had to transfer more money than it has in the Capital Reserve Account to the Financing Account to cover an increase in expected losses on insured loans, it could draw on its permanent and indefinite budget authority to make this transfer without additional congressional action.[45] To date, FHA has never had to use this authority. However, there has been increased concern that FHA might need to use this authority in the wake of the most recent actuarial report on the MMI Fund, discussed in detail in the **Appendix**, which estimated that the MMI Fund does not currently have enough funds on hand to pay for all of its expected future losses on the loans that it currently insures.

If FHA did draw on Treasury to make a required transfer of funds to the Financing Account, these funds would not be spent immediately. Rather, they would be held in the Financing Account, and used to pay claims to lenders only if the rest of the funds in the Financing Account were exhausted. If economic conditions and loan performance improved, or if loans insured in the future brought in enough money to both cover their own costs and pay for past loans that defaulted, it would be possible that any money received from Treasury would never actually be spent and could be returned to Treasury. On the other hand, if future insured loans did not bring in enough funds to cover losses on past loans, or if economic conditions and loan performance deteriorated further, any funds received from Treasury could eventually be spent to pay actual claims.

When the FY2013 President's Budget request was released in February 2012, it indicated that FHA might need to draw on its permanent and indefinite budget authority with Treasury to make such a transfer of funds during FY2012. The budget request indicated that more funds than were currently available in the Capital Reserve Account were likely to be needed to be transferred to the Financing Account in FY2012 to cover another increase in expected future losses. To cover this transfer, the budget included $688 million in mandatory appropriations, representing a draw on the permanent and indefinite budget authority provided to FHA.[46]

---

[44] These numbers represent total amortized insurance-in-force for the MMI Fund. Figures come from FHA's *Annual Report to Congress on the Financial Status of the MMI Fund*, FY2009, p. 17, and the *Annual Report to Congress on the Financial Status of the MMI Fund, FY2012*, p. 35.

[45] The credit subsidy rate re-estimates are included as part of the President's budget that is usually released in February of each year. Any required transfer of funds between the Financing Account and the Capital Reserve Account usually occurs in May or June, but can happen as late as September.

[46] *The Appendix, Budget of the United States Government, Fiscal Year 2013*, p. 636, http://www.whitehouse.gov/sites/default/files/omb/budget/fy2013/assets/hud.pdf.

However, after the budget request was released, FHA stated that it no longer expected to need that money from Treasury in FY2012 largely because of money it would receive from recent settlements with large mortgage companies related to claims that the companies did not adhere to FHA requirements in originating and servicing loans.[47] FHA had also made various policy changes (such as mortgage insurance premium increases for new borrowers) that, along with the settlement actions, were expected to bring in enough funds to cover any required transfer of funds from the Capital Reserve Account to the Financing Account in FY2012. However, if expected losses on currently insured loans continue to increase in future years, and if enough new funds do not come into the MMI Fund in the form of premiums or other revenue to cover any such increases in expected losses, then FHA could have to draw on Treasury in a future year.

Annual Actuarial Review and 2% Capital Ratio Requirement

Each year, FHA contracts with an independent actuary to conduct an actuarial review of the MMI Fund as mandated by Congress. This review analyzes FHA's financial position by estimating the amount of funds that it currently has on hand and the net amount (in present value terms) that FHA expects to earn or lose in the future on loans that it currently insures. It then adds these numbers together to compute the "economic value" of the MMI Fund, which is basically the amount of funds that the MMI Fund would be projected to have on hand after paying for all of its future expected losses, assuming that it did not insure any more loans going forward. This actuarial review is separate from the budget process, and uses somewhat different economic

assumptions than those used in the federal budget.

Congress also mandates that FHA meet a 2% capital reserve requirement, which means

> ### Where to Find FHA Reports on the MMI Fund
>
> The FHA reports discussed in this section, including the annual actuarial report and the annual report to Congress on the financial status of the MMI Fund, can be accessed from HUD's Office of Housing Reading Room webpage at http://portal.hud.gov/hudportal/HUD?src=/program_offices/housing/hsgrroom.

that the economic value of the MMI Fund—the amount of funds that the MMI Fund would have remaining after paying all expected future losses—must be at least 2% of the total dollar volume of mortgages that FHA currently insures. The capital ratio is calculated on the basis of the actuarial report. The capital ratio fell below this 2% requirement in FY2009, and has continued to fall since then.

The FY2012 annual actuarial review was released in November 2012, and it showed that the economic value of the MMI Fund is currently estimated to be negative.[48] A negative economic value means that the MMI Fund does not currently have enough funds on hand to pay for all of its expected future losses over the life of the loans that it currently insures. It does not mean that FHA does not have funds to pay claims today, but it raises concerns that FHA might run out of funds to pay claims in the future. The projected losses on the loans currently insured by FHA will be realized over the life of those loans, rather than all at once, potentially giving FHA time to

---

[47] Written Testimony of Shaun Donovan, Secretary of U.S. Department of Housing and Urban Development, Hearing before the Subcommittee on Transportation, Housing and Urban Development, and Related Agencies, U.S. House of Representatives Committee on Appropriations on "FY2013 Budget Request for the Department of Housing and Urban Development," March 21, 2012, p. 7, http://appropriations.house.gov/uploadedfiles/hhrg-112-ap20-wstate-sdonovan-20120321.pdf.

[48] The annual actuarial reviews can be found on HUD's website at http://portal.hud.gov/hudportal/HUD?mode=dispcontent&id=HSG_ACTRMENU_10941&type=HUDGOV_HTML&rsm=Latest&width=664.

---

increase the funds that it has on hand before these projected losses are realized. Whether or not the MMI Fund will ever actually run out of money to pay claims depends on factors such as whether the projections of the performance of FHA-insured loans are accurate and whether the MMI Fund is able to build enough additional capital resources over time, such as through additional premium revenue from newly insured mortgages, to pay for these expected claims.

Because the economic value of the MMI Fund is estimated to be negative, the capital ratio is also estimated to be negative. This represents the first time that the MMI Fund has been estimated to have a negative capital ratio since it first met the mandated 2% capital ratio requirement in the mid-1990s.

Although the results of the actuarial review raise serious concerns about the financial soundness of the MMI Fund going forward, the results of the actuarial review do not determine whether or not FHA will need to draw on its permanent and indefinite budget authority with Treasury for funds to hold against expected future losses or to pay claims. That is determined as part of the re-estimate process that is done as part of the federal budgeting process each year, which was described in the previous section. The actuarial review, the capital ratio, and the results of the FY2012 actuarial report are all described in more detail in the **Appendix**.

The FY2012 actuarial review estimates that, based on current assumptions, the MMI Fund could regain a positive economic value in FY2014, and could regain a capital ratio of 2% by FY2017. Unlike the estimate of the FY2012 economic value of the MMI Fund, which assumes that FHA will not insure any new loans, the estimates of the future economic value of the MMI Fund do take into account the expected economic value of loans that FHA will insure in the future. However, some have raised concerns that, for a variety of reasons, the estimates of the MMI Fund's future economic value could be too optimistic.

For example, some have expressed concern that FHA is trying to grow itself out of its financial problems by insuring a higher dollar volume of loans and relying on the premium revenue that those loans will bring in to restore the MMI Fund's economic value and capital ratio. This could be a problem if these loans do not perform well, or if FHA is relying on maintaining a relatively high market share even though its future market role is uncertain. Some also note that, given that most past cohorts of loans insured by FHA have performed less well than initially anticipated, it would be reasonable to expect loans insured in the future to also perform less well than currently anticipated.[49] They suggest policy changes including increasing downpayment or credit score requirements for FHA-insured borrowers and changing the way that FHA estimates the value of the loans that it insures.[50] Others have suggested that the actuarial estimates might rely on overly optimistic assumptions about house price trajectories and other factors, leading to an overestimate of the economic value of the MMI Fund.[51]

---

[49] For example, see Gyourko, Joseph, "Is FHA the Next Housing Bailout?," American Enterprise Institute Working Paper #2011-06, November 2011, http://real.wharton.upenn.edu/~gyourko/Working%20Papers/FHA-AEI_11%2015_for%20posting-final_jgedits.pdf.

[50] For example, see U.S. Congress, House Committee on Financial Services, Subcommittee on Insurance, Housing and Community Opportunity, *Legislative Proposals to Determine the Future Role of FHA, RHS, and GNMA in the Single- and Multi-Family Mortgage Markets, Part 1*, 112th Congress, 1st. sess., May 25, 2011, H. Hrg. 112-32 (Washington: GPO, 2012), http://financialservices.house.gov/uploadedfiles/112-32.pdf. In particular, see the testimony of Mark Calabria, Director of Financial Regulation Studies at the Cato Institute.

[51] For example, see Wallison, Peter J. and Edward J. Pinto, American Enterprise Institute, "Bet the house: why the FHA is going (for) broke," January 19, 2012, http://www.aei.org/outlook/economics/financial-services/housing-(continued...)

In response to these criticisms, FHA argues that the recent increase in its share of the mortgage market has been driven by market forces, namely, by lenders and private mortgage insurers tightening their credit standards, leaving FHA as the only option for some borrowers. FHA also maintains that recent increases in mortgage insurance premiums and in the credit quality of the loans that it insures will mean that the loans that it insured in more recent years will perform better than loans insured in past years. Finally, FHA responds to criticism that its house price and other forecasts are too optimistic by noting that the independent actuary uses standard forecasts developed by independent private firms.[52]

FHA acknowledges that the actuarial position of the MMI Fund is cause for concern. To address this concern, it has made a number of policy changes in recent years aimed at addressing the health of the MMI Fund, many of which are discussed in the next section, and has indicated that it is considering a variety of additional policy changes. Nevertheless, many policymakers and others argue that FHA has not gone far enough with the changes it has undertaken to date and have called for additional action.

Selected Recent FHA Policy Changes

In the current environment, FHA faces an increased tension between fulfilling its traditional role of facilitating the provision of mortgage credit to underserved borrowers and supporting the currently fragile housing market, on the one hand, and safeguarding the health of the MMI Fund on the other. With this tension in mind, FHA has made several changes to its single-family insurance programs since FY2010. These changes generally attempt to increase FHA's cash reserves, to decrease the riskiness of the mortgages it insures, or both. FHA had the authority to make some of these changes administratively, through policy guidance or rulemaking procedures, while others required congressional action.

In general, most of the changes that FHA has made or could make—including increasing premiums and strengthening underwriting criteria—impact the risk profile of future loans that FHA will insure rather than loans that FHA has already insured. FHA has fewer options at its disposal for making changes that will reduce its risk related to loans that it already insures. However, it has taken some steps, such as more aggressively holding lenders accountable for loans they originated that did not meet FHA's criteria, that address past loans as well as future loans.

This section describes major underwriting and risk management changes that FHA has announced or implemented in recent years, including new policy changes that FHA announced when the FY2012 actuarial review was released. It also discusses changes that have been required by Congress, and additional legislative proposals for further changes aimed at protecting the financial stability of the FHA single-family loan program.

(...continued)

finance/bet-the-house-why-the-fha-is-going-for-broke/.

[52] U.S. Department of Housing and Urban Development, "Myths and Facts Regarding the FHA Single Family Loan Guarantee Portfolio," http://portal.hud.gov/hudportal/documents/huddoc?id=MythsandFactsLoanPortfolio.pdf.

Mortgage Origination and Underwriting Changes

Some of the changes that FHA has initiated over the past few years involve increasing the premiums that borrowers pay for FHA-insured mortgages and strengthening FHA's underwriting guidelines for its single-family program. The premium increases are intended to ensure that FHA is charging enough for its insurance to cover its potential costs, as well as to build up additional funds that can be used to pay for higher-than-expected losses on loans that FHA insures. The underwriting changes are aimed at making FHA-insured mortgages less likely to default, and therefore likely to result in fewer claims that FHA has to pay. However, as a result of these underwriting changes and the premium increases, some prospective homebuyers may find that they are no longer eligible for FHA insurance, or that FHA-insured mortgages are no longer an affordable option.

Mortgage Insurance Premium Increases

Borrowers of FHA-insured mortgages pay both *upfront* and *annual* mortgage insurance premiums. The upfront premium is paid when the loan is originated, and the annual premiums are paid each year thereafter. These premiums comprise a large portion of the cash flow into the MMI Fund. The maximum levels of both the upfront and annual mortgage insurance premiums are set in statute, but FHA can administratively set the actual premiums it charges, as long as it does not exceed the statutory maximum.[53]

Since April 2010, FHA has made a series of changes to the premiums it charges. Most of these changes have affected the annual premium, rather than the upfront premium. For the most part, these changes have been made administratively by FHA, although Congress required an increase in the annual mortgage insurance premium of 10 basis points (one-tenth of one percent) in the Temporary Payroll Tax Cut Continuation Act of 2011 (P.L. 112-78). Congress has also passed legislation raising the maximum statutory annual premium that FHA is allowed to charge.[54]

Table 3 shows the current mortgage insurance premiums charged by FHA since June 11, 2012, as well as the maximum premium that FHA is currently allowed to charge by statute. The upfront premium for FHA-insured loans is 1.75% of the loan amount (the same amount that FHA was charging at the beginning of 2010). For most mortgages, the annual premiums are 1.20% for mortgages with loan-to-value ratios of 95% or below, and 1.25% for mortgages with loan-to-value ratios above 95%. (These are increased from annual premiums of 0.50% and 0.55%, respectively, at the beginning of 2010.) However, FHA has also begun charging higher annual mortgage insurance premiums for mortgages with initial principal balances above $625,500, the conforming loan limit for Fannie Mae and Freddie Mac mortgages in high-cost areas.[55] For mortgages with principal balances above $625,500, the annual mortgage insurance premium will

---

[53] The maximum mortgage insurance premium amounts that FHA can charge are codified at 12 U.S.C. § 1709(c)(2).

[54] When FHA began raising its premiums in 2010, it was charging the maximum annual mortgage insurance premium allowed by statute. Therefore, FHA raised the upfront premium, and asked Congress for authority to increase the annual mortgage insurance premium. Congress passed legislation increasing the maximum annual mortgage insurance premium that FHA can charge in August 2010 (P.L. 111-229), and FHA subsequently raised the annual premiums while lowering the upfront premium to a lower level than it had been charging at the beginning of 2010. Since that time, FHA has since increased the upfront premium back to what it was charging at the beginning of 2010.

[55] The maximum loan amount that FHA will insure in high-cost areas is currently $729,750.

---

be 1.45% for mortgages with loan-to-value ratios of 95% or below, and 1.50% for mortgages with loan-to-value ratios above 95%.

Table 3. FHA Single-Family Forward Mortgage Insurance Premiums (MIPs)

As of June 11, 2012

Loan-to-Value Ratio	Statutory Maximum Upfront MIP	Current Upfront MIP	Statutory Maximum Annual MIP	Current Annual MIP
Loans with Principal Balances at or below $625,500				
Less than or equal to 95%	3%	1.75%	1.5%	1.20%
Above 95%	3%	1.75%	1.55%	1.25%
Loans with Principal Balances above $625,500				
Less than or equal to 95%	3%	1.75%	1.5%	1.45%
Above 95%	3%	1.75%	1.55%	1.50%

Source: Table created by CRS based on FHA Mortgagee Letter 12-4.

Notes: Different premiums apply to certain types of mortgages, such as streamline refinances or mortgages with shorter loan terms.

After the FY2012 annual actuarial report was released, FHA announced that it planned to increase annual mortgage insurance premiums by an additional 10 basis points, or one-tenth of a percentage point. (See the "Additional Changes Announced with the FY2012 Actuarial Review" section of this report.) This announced change will be in addition to the premiums reflected in the above table.

Increasing the premiums that FHA charges is likely to result in more revenue coming into the MMI Fund, unless the increase in premiums reduces the volume of new FHA-insured mortgages by a great enough amount to counteract the increase in premiums. Increased premiums have the potential to reduce FHA's role in the mortgage market by pricing some borrowers out of the market for FHA-insured mortgages or by making private mortgage insurance more competitive with FHA insurance for some borrowers. Raising premiums might also better align the pricing of FHA-insured mortgages with their risk, although in some cases raising the premiums has the potential to actually increase the riskiness of the mortgage. For example, because the upfront premium is generally financed into the mortgage, increasing the upfront mortgage insurance premium has the effect of reducing a borrower's initial equity in the home (by increasing the initial loan balance and/or reducing the amount of funds that a borrower has available for a downpayment).

Changes to Downpayment and Credit Score Requirements

Another change that FHA has undertaken is increasing the required downpayment for borrowers with lower credit scores. Prior to making this change, the required FHA downpayment was 3.5% for most borrowers, except that borrowers with credit scores below 500 were required to make a downpayment of at least 10%.

Beginning on October 4, 2010, FHA requires a downpayment of at least 10% from borrowers with credit scores between 500 and 579, while the downpayment requirement of 3.5% remains in place for borrowers with credit scores of 580 or above. FHA has expressed concerns about risk layering, suggesting that loans are at a higher risk of default when a loan exhibits multiple risk factors (such as a lower credit score combined with a higher loan-to-value ratio), rather than just one risk factor.[56] The increased downpayment for borrowers with credit scores below 580 is aimed at addressing that concern.

Furthermore, FHA no longer insures loans made to borrowers with credit scores below 500.[57] FHA has stated that it has not insured many loans where the borrower's credit score is below 500, but the loans that it does insure with borrower credit scores below that threshold perform appreciably less well than loans to borrowers with higher credit scores.[58] Since it currently insures few loans that fit these criteria, FHA believes these changes will affect a relatively small number of potential borrowers.

Table 4 summarizes the current downpayment requirements.

Table 4. Required Downpayments for FHA-Insured Mortgages
Effective as of October 4, 2010

Credit Score	Previous Required Downpayment	Current Required Downpayment
Below 500	10%	Not eligible for FHA insurance
500-579	3.5%	10%
580 or above	3.5%	3.5%

Source: FHA Mortgagee Letter 10-29

FHA is able to undertake these changes through rulemaking procedures, and it published a Federal Register notice on July 15, 2010, soliciting public comment on these and other changes.[59] HUD then issued a Final Rule addressing only this change on September 3, 2010,[60] along with administrative guidance providing additional information on the implementation of this change.[61]

---

[56] Department of Housing and Urban Development, "Federal Housing Administration Risk Management Initiatives: Reduction of Seller Concessions and New Loan-to-Value and Credit Score Requirements," 75 *Federal Register* 41218, July 15, 2010.

[57] U.S. Department of Housing and Urban Development, FHA Mortgagee Letter 10-29, "Minimum Credit Scores and Loan-to-Value Ratios," September 3, 2010, http://www.hud.gov/offices/adm/hudclips/letters/mortgagee/files/10-29ml.pdf.

[58] U.S. Department of Housing and Urban Development, "Federal Housing Administration Risk Management Initiatives: Reduction of Seller Concessions and New Loan-to-Value and Credit Score Requirements," 75 *Federal Register* 41221, July 15, 2010.

[59] Department of Housing and Urban Development, "Federal Housing Administration Risk Management Initiatives: Reduction of Seller Concessions and New Loan-to-Value and Credit Score Requirements," 75 *Federal Register* 41217-41225, July 15, 2010.

[60] Department of Housing and Urban Development, "Federal Housing Administration Risk Management Initiatives: New Loan-to-Value and Credit Score Requirements," 75 *Federal Register* 54020-54023, September 3, 2010.

[61] Department of Housing and Urban Development, FHA Mortgagee Letter 10-29, "Minimum Credit Scores and Loan-to-Value Ratios," September 3, 2010, http://www.hud.gov/offices/adm/hudclips/letters/mortgagee/files/10-29ml.pdf.

Figure 3 illustrates the distribution of borrowers' credit scores by dollar volume of loans insured by FHA in each year between 2006 and 2011. The percentage of the total dollar volume of FHA-insured loans made to borrowers with lower credit scores decreased over this time period, and the percentage of loans made to borrowers with higher credit scores increased, particularly in the 2009-2011 time period. This outcome reflects the general tightening of mortgage credit in the aftermath of the housing bubble, when even some borrowers with strong credit scores might have had difficulty accessing private alternatives for mortgage insurance, and some borrowers with lower credit scores might not have been able to obtain a mortgage at all. In addition, the increase in the loan limits for FHA-insured mortgages, particularly in high-cost areas, may have made FHA-insured loans an option for more borrowers with better credit scores who live in those areas.

Since 2009, well under 10% of FHA-insured loans (by dollar volume) have been made to borrowers with credit scores below 600; in earlier years, higher proportions of the dollar volume of loans insured in each year were made to such borrowers, including over 30% in 2007. Given this shift towards FHA serving a higher proportion of borrowers with better credit scores in recent years, it is likely that the downpayment changes for the borrowers with the lowest credit scores will affect a relatively small share of potential borrowers in the near future. However, if borrowers with higher credit scores begin turning to the conventional mortgage market and private mortgage insurance, and if FHA seeks to return to a more traditional role of insuring a higher proportion of mortgages made to borrowers with lower credit scores, it is possible that more borrowers who traditionally might have sought out FHA-insured mortgages could find themselves unable to qualify based on their credit scores and the higher downpayment requirements.

Figure 3. Percentage of Newly Originated FHA-Insured Mortgages (by Dollar Volume) by Borrower FICO Score

FY2006-FY2012

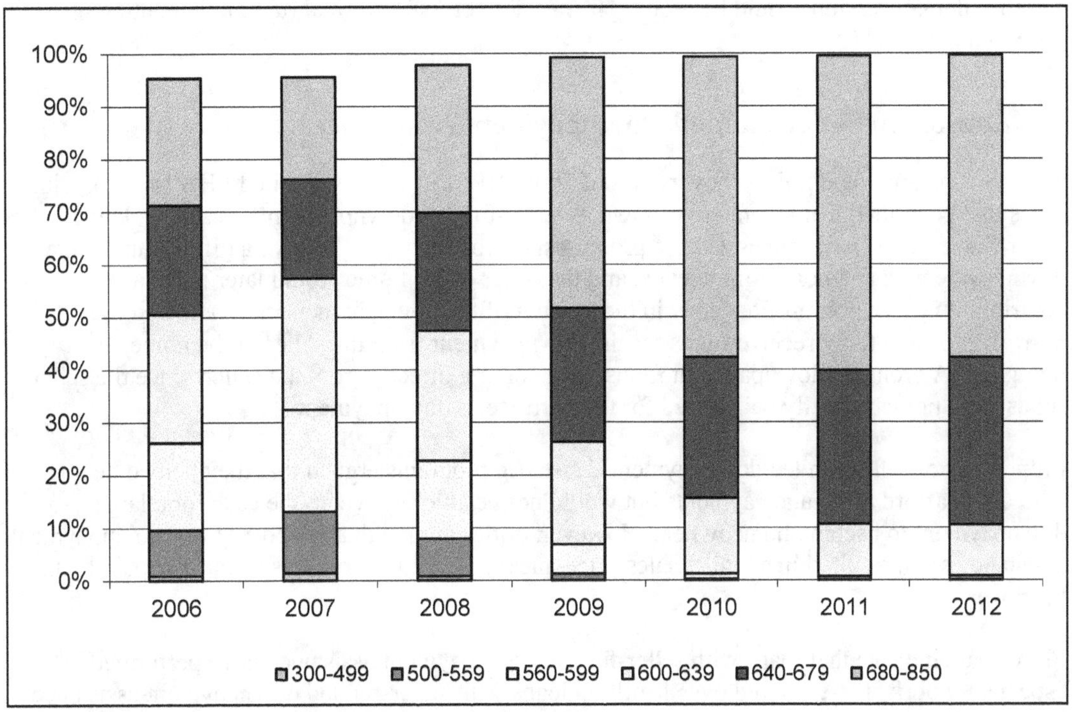

Source: Figure created by CRS based on data from Integrated Financial Engineering, Inc., *Actuarial Review of the Federal Housing Administration Mutual Mortgage Insurance Fund (Excluding HECMs) for Fiscal Year 2012*, prepared for the Department of Housing and Urban Development, page 48.

Notes: Missing data in each year ranges from a low of 0.31% in FY2012 to a high of 4.66% in FY2006.

Proposed Reduction in Allowable Seller Concessions

FHA has also proposed reducing the amount of allowable seller concessions to 3% of the lesser of the home's sale price or appraised value, down from 6%. Seller concessions are any contribution to the borrower's closing costs made by the seller or any other interested third party. FHA maintains that this change is in line with industry standards for loans with loan-to-value ratios similar to FHA's, and that FHA-insured loans with higher amounts of seller concessions have performed more poorly in the past.[62] While higher amounts of seller concessions will not be absolutely prohibited, any amount of seller concessions above the 3% threshold will result in a reduction of the maximum loan amount that FHA will insure. FHA proposed this change in the same Federal Register notice in which it announced its new credit score and loan-to-value ratio requirements, and solicited public comment until August 16, 2010.

---

[62] Department of Housing and Urban Development, "Federal Housing Administration Risk Management Initiatives: Reduction of Seller Concessions and New Loan-to-Value and Credit Score Requirements," 75 *Federal Register* 41220, July 15, 2010. For example, FHA notes that seller concessions are capped at 4% of the sales price for loans guaranteed by the VA.

In February 2012, FHA issued a notice revising its proposal and soliciting comments on the revisions.[63] Specifically, FHA proposed limiting seller concessions to the greater of $6,000 or 3% of the lesser of the home's purchase price or appraised value. The notice also limits the items for which seller concessions could be used. FHA has not yet issued a final rule implementing this proposed change.

Prohibition on Seller-Funded Downpayment Assistance

The Housing and Economic Recovery Act of 2008 (P.L. 110-289) prohibited FHA from insuring loans that benefitted from a practice known as seller-funded downpayment assistance. Under seller-funded downpayment assistance programs, borrowers would receive a gift of funds for a downpayment from a non-profit agency, and the seller of the home would later make a contribution to the non-profit agency in the amount of the downpayment. This allowed the borrower to essentially receive funds for the downpayment from the seller of the home, even though FHA prohibits downpayment funds from coming directly from the seller, since the seller's funds were not technically being used for the borrower's downpayment.[64]

Proponents of seller-funded downpayment assistance programs argued that they helped people who could afford mortgage payments but would not be able to save up the cash for a large downpayment to become homeowners. However, critics argued that the cost of this downpayment assistance often resulted in a higher sales price, meaning that the cost was ultimately paid by the borrower.

FHA's data indicate that loans with seller-funded downpayment assistance have performed especially poorly. FHA insured over 1 million loans with seller-funded downpayment assistance between 1998 and 2009, and according to FHA data, these loans have had claim rates as high as three times those of other FHA-insured loans. As of FY2010, FHA reported that 34% of seller-funded downpayment assisted loans that were still active were seriously delinquent, along with 12% of refinanced seller-funded downpayment assisted loans.[65] FHA indicates that the MMI Fund's economic value would have been estimated to be positive in FY2012 if FHA had not insured these loans, and that it expects the seller-funded downpayment assistance loans to ultimately cost the MMI Fund over $15 billion.[66]

---

[63] Department of Housing and Urban Development, "Federal Housing Administration (FHA) Risk Management Initiatives: Revised Seller Concessions," 77 *Federal Register* 10695-10707, February 23, 2012.

[64] For more information on seller-funded downpayment assistance, see CRS Report RS22934, *Treatment of Seller-Funded Downpayment Assistance in FHA-Insured Home Loans*, by Bruce E. Foote, and Government Accountability Office, *Mortgage Financing: Additional Action Needed to Manage Risks of FHA-Insured Loans with Down Payment Assistance*, November 2005, http://www.gao.gov/assets/250/248463.pdf.

[65] U.S. Department of Housing and Urban Development, *Annual Report to Congress Regarding the Financial Status of the Mutual Mortgage Insurance Fund, Fiscal Year 2010*, November 15, 2010, pages 24-25, http://portal.hud.gov/hudportal/documents/huddoc?id=DOC_12561.pdf.

[66] U.S. Department of Housing and Urban Development, *Annual Report to Congress on the Financial Status of the Mutual Mortgage Insurance Fund, FY2012*, November 16, 2012, p. 25, http://portal.hud.gov/hudportal/documents/huddoc?id=F12MMIFundRepCong111612.pdf.

Lender Monitoring and Risk Management

In order to originate mortgages that will be insured by FHA, a lender has to be approved by FHA. FHA-approved lenders must meet certain criteria, and the loans that they submit for FHA insurance must meet FHA's standards. Loans that do not meet FHA's requirements, but are submitted for FHA insurance, can cost FHA money if they default in the future. Therefore, FHA can take a number of actions against lenders if they do not adhere to FHA's requirements.

In recent years, FHA has taken a number of steps to increase its oversight of FHA-approved lenders and otherwise manage its risk. Congress also strengthened FHA's authority related to FHA-insured lenders through certain provisions enacted in the Helping Families Save Their Homes Act of 2009 (P.L. 111-22).[67]

Net Worth Requirements for FHA-Insured Lenders

In April 2010, HUD published a final rule with request for comments making several changes related to FHA's risk management.[68] This final rule increased the net worth requirements for FHA-approved lenders to $1 million, with at least 20% of that amount held in cash or its equivalent, effective May 20, 2010, for new applicants and effective May 20, 2011, for lenders who were already FHA-approved. By May 20, 2013, FHA-insured lenders will be required to have a net worth of $1 million plus an additional 1% of the volume of FHA-insured loans originated, underwritten, purchased, or serviced by the lender in the previous fiscal year, up to a maximum net worth requirement of $2.5 million. Twenty percent of this net worth requirement must be held in liquid assets.

FHA's rationale for this change is that it is necessary to ensure that FHA-approved lenders have sufficient liquidity to withstand market fluctuations and any related losses that they might incur. FHA also notes that the net worth requirements had not been increased since 1993, and therefore this change was necessary to account for inflation. However, some lenders have raised concerns that the increased net worth requirements could be burdensome for some lenders, and in particular could be more difficult for small lenders to meet than large lenders. Some have also raised concerns that increased costs to lenders of complying with these requirements could be passed on to borrowers.[69]

---

[67] See FHA Mortgagee Letter 09-31, "Strengthening Counterparty Risk Management," September 18, 2009, available at http://www.hud.gov/offices/adm/hudclips/letters/mortgagee/2009ml.cfm, for a description of the provisions related to FHA lender monitoring that were enacted in the Helping Families Save Their Homes Act.

[68] U.S. Department of Housing and Urban Development, "Federal Housing Administration: Continuation of FHA Reform: Strengthening Risk Management Through Responsible FHA-Approved Lenders," 75 *Federal Register* 20718-20735, April 20, 2010. A Final Rule providing clarification and correction was published in August 2012. See U.S. Department of Housing and Urban Development, "Federal Housing Administration: Strengthening Risk Management Through Responsible FHA-Approved Lenders," 77 *Federal Register* 51465-51469, August 24, 2012.

[69] For example, see the discussion of the comments submitted on these changes in the April 2010 Final Rule with request for comment at 75 *Federal Register* 20722. Also, see the discussion of these changes and the concerns that some industry participants have raised in Government Accountability Office, "Federal Housing Administration: Improvements Needed in Risk Assessment and Human Capital Management," November 2011, pages 28-29, http://www.gao.gov/assets/590/586116.pdf.

Elimination of Approval of Loan Correspondents

In the same rule, FHA also made changes in its approval and monitoring of entities, such as mortgage brokers, that partner with lenders to originate FHA-insured loans. As noted, in order to make FHA-insured loans, a lender must be approved by FHA. FHA had issued a different type of approval to entities that partner with lenders to originate FHA-insured loans, and it referred to these entities as loan correspondents. The entities it referred to as loan correspondents perform many functions related to originating a mortgage, but cannot underwrite FHA-insured mortgages, nor can they service or own such mortgages. Full-fledged FHA participating lenders, on the other hand, are authorized to perform all origination functions including underwriting, and can own and service FHA-insured loans.

In the April 2010 final rule, FHA announced that it would no longer give FHA approval to loan correspondents. Entities that were previously approved as loan correspondents can continue to participate in the process of originating FHA-insured loans by becoming what FHA will now call third-party originators (TPOs) and partnering with an FHA-approved lender. The FHA-approved lender, not FHA, is now responsible for overseeing TPOs that it partners with and ensuring that they comply with all FHA requirements. TPOs can also apply to become FHA-approved lenders if they are able to undertake the underwriting, servicing, and ownership functions of FHA-approved lenders.

FHA's rationale for this change is that the lender responsible for underwriting, owning, or servicing the mortgage bears the most responsibility for the mortgage, and therefore FHA's approval and oversight resources should be focused on these entities rather than on TPOs. By no longer issuing approval to loan correspondents/TPOs, FHA can focus more of its oversight efforts and resources on the lenders that underwrite, own, and service FHA-insured mortgages. FHA believes that it is appropriate for FHA-insured lenders to bear the responsibility for ensuring that TPOs comply with FHA's requirements, since it is already the responsibility of lenders to make sure that the FHA-insured loans that they originate meet FHA's standards. However, some industry participants have raised concerns that removing the separate approval of loan correspondents could make it more difficult for some entities, including small banks, to participate in FHA programs, or could increase costs to FHA-approved lenders who will need to hire new staff to perform functions for which it used to rely on loan correspondents. Some have also raised concerns about removing FHA oversight of TPOs entirely, and noted that this change could increase risk to the insurance fund if FHA-approved lenders do not adequately oversee TPOs.[70]

FHA stopped approving new applications for approval as loan correspondents on May 30, 2010; loan correspondents who were already approved retained that approval through December 31, 2010. As of January 1, 2011, the entities now known as TPOs are no longer allowed to close loans in their own name. This is because, by statute, loans must be closed by FHA-approved lenders, and TPOs are not eligible for FHA approval. However, FHA has said that it will continue to examine the issue of prohibiting TPOs from closing loans in their own names.

---

[70] For example, see the discussion of the comments submitted on these changes in the April 2010 Final Rule with request for comment at 75 Federal Register 20723-20724.

Chief Risk Officer

In September 2009, FHA announced that it was appointing a Chief Risk Officer for the first time in its history. The Chief Risk Officer now has coordinated responsibility for overseeing all of the risk management functions across FHA programs.[71] Previously, responsibility for managing risk was spread across different program offices. FHA believes that a single Chief Risk Officer can take a more consolidated approach to managing risk in FHA's programs, which could reduce its exposure to risk and therefore strengthen the MMI Fund.

Increased Oversight of FHA-Approved Lenders

FHA monitors approved lenders that originate FHA-insured mortgages, and FHA can take certain administrative actions against lenders who submit mortgages for insurance that do not meet FHA guidelines or otherwise fail to adhere to FHA standards. These actions include suspending lenders from FHA programs or terminating their approval to originate FHA-insured mortgages entirely, imposing civil money penalties, or other actions. HUD's Mortgagee Review Board (MRB) reviews cases of lenders not complying with FHA requirements and enters into agreements to bring lenders into compliance or imposes penalties where necessary.[72] HUD can also refer certain cases to the Justice Department for prosecution under federal statutes such as the False Claims Act or the Program Fraud Civil Remedies Act.

FHA has increasingly taken action against lenders who originated mortgages that did not adhere to FHA guidelines in recent years. Between 2009 and mid-2011, the MRB took over 2,000 actions against lenders.[73] FHA has also pursued some high-profile cases against lenders who had high FHA claim rates due to poor underwriting or otherwise did not follow FHA guidelines.[74]

In addition to increasing actions against lenders under its existing authority, FHA has also implemented changes through regulation to strengthen its authority to require certain lenders to compensate FHA for insurance claims paid on mortgages that do not meet its requirements. FHA-approved lenders that are also approved to originate FHA-insured mortgages under a certain process[75] may be required by statute to compensate, or indemnify, FHA in cases of fraud or misrepresentation on the part of the lender or for claims paid on mortgages that did not comply

---

[71] U.S. Department of Housing and Urban Development, "FHA Announces Credit Policy Changes, Adding Chief Risk Officer," press release, September 18, 2009, http://portal.hud.gov/hudportal/HUD?src=/press/press_releases_media_advisories/2009/HUDNo.09-177.

[72] For more information on the Mortgagee Review Board, see HUD's website at http://portal.hud.gov/hudportal/HUD?src=/program_offices/housing/sfh/mrb/mrbabout.

[73] U.S. Department of Housing and Urban Development, "FHA's Mortgagee Review Board Takes Action Against 240 Lenders," press release, July 29, 2011, http://portal.hud.gov/hudportal/HUD?src=/press/press_releases_media_advisories/2011/HUDNo.11-161.

[74] For examples of different types of actions HUD has taken against certain lenders, see HUD press release 09-217, *FHA and Ginnie Mae Take Action Against Lend America*, November 30, 2009, http://portal.hud.gov/hudportal/HUD?src=/press/press_releases_media_advisories/2009/HUDNo.09-217 and HUD press release 12-163, *Manhattan U.S. Attorney Files Mortgage Fraud Lawsuit Against Wells Fargo Bank, N.A. Seeking Hundreds of Millions of Dollars in Damages for Fraudulently Certified Loans*, October 9, 2012, http://portal.hud.gov/hudportal/HUD?src=/press/press_releases_media_advisories/2012/HUDNo.12-163.

[75] FHA can require indemnification from lenders who originate loans under the Lender Insurance process. Certain high-performing FHA-approved lenders can be approved to originate loans under the Lender Insurance process, which allows them to endorse loans for FHA insurance without a pre-insurance endorsement review by FHA.

---

with FHA loan requirements.[76] In October 2010, FHA issued a proposed rule that would clarify these requirements,[77] and in January 2012, FHA issued a final rule implementing these updated requirements.[78]

FHA is also seeking statutory changes that would increase FHA's indemnification authority by extending the indemnification provisions to other FHA-approved lenders, as well as changes that would expand FHA's authority to terminate the approval of lenders under certain circumstances. Such provisions have been included in FHA reform legislation that has been considered by Congress; examples of such bills are noted in the "Selected Legislative Proposals" section of this report.

Additional Changes Announced with the FY2012 Actuarial Review

When the FY2012 annual actuarial review was released in November 2012, it estimated that the MMI Fund does not currently have enough funds on hand to cover all of its expected future losses on the loans that it currently insures. (See the "Annual Actuarial Review and 2% Capital Ratio Requirement" section of this report for an overview, and the **Appendix** for a more in-depth discussion of the actuarial review.) The results of the actuarial review suggest that FHA could at some point need funds from Treasury to hold in reserve against expected future losses. However, the need for funds from Treasury would be determined by the annual budget re-estimate process, not the actuarial review.

Given the results of the FY2012 actuarial review, FHA announced a number of additional policy changes intended to avoid the need to draw funds from Treasury to hold in reserve against expected future losses. Broadly speaking, these policy changes can be divided into changes that affect existing loans, and those that will affect new loans insured by FHA in the future. These changes are briefly described below.

In addition to the policy changes described here, FHA also indicated that it could announce additional policy changes in the future, including changes related to FHA-insured reverse mortgages. FHA has also requested legislative action to provide it with additional authority to oversee lenders. Specifically, it has requested increased authority to require compensation for insurance claims from lenders in certain situations, increased authority to terminate the approval lenders that are not performing well, and greater authority to transfer mortgage servicing rights to servicers that are better at utilizing loss mitigation actions to reduce losses to the MMI Fund.[79] These changes would require legislation, and are not within FHA's existing authority.

---

[76] 12 U.S.C. § 1715z-21(c)

[77] Department of Housing and Urban Development, "Federal Housing Administration (FHA) Single Family Lender Insurance Process: Eligibility, Indemnification, and Termination," 75 *Federal Register* 62335-62342, October 8, 2010.

[78] Department of Housing and Urban Development, "Federal Housing Administration (FHA) Single Family Lender Insurance Process: Eligibility, Indemnification, and Termination," 77 *Federal Register* 3598-3605, January 25, 2012.

[79] The increased legislative authorities that FHA is requesting are described on pages 57-58 of FHA's *FY2012 Annual Report to Congress on the Financial Status of the MMI Fund*.

Changes Affecting Loans Already Insured

FHA announced a number of policy changes that will affect loans that it already insures. These changes mostly have to do with how FHA deals with defaulted FHA-insured mortgages or foreclosed properties. The actions announced by FHA include the following:

- Expanding a pilot program through which FHA sells FHA-insured mortgages in default to investors.

- Making changes to loss mitigation procedures designed to help more borrowers keep their homes and, consequently, reduce claims paid on foreclosures.[80]

- Streamlining its short sale policy to try to increase the number of mortgages that are sold in a short sale rather than a foreclosure. Since homes that go through short sales often sell for less of a loss than a foreclosure, FHA expects that facilitating more short sales will reduce losses to the MMI Fund.

- Expanding a pilot program through which foreclosed homes are sold by lenders rather than being conveyed to FHA to sell. This is expected to reduce losses to the MMI Fund by reducing the costs to FHA of managing foreclosed properties before they are sold.

Changes Affecting Future Loans

FHA also announced a number of policy changes that will affect mortgages that it insures in the future. First, it announced that it would increase the annual premiums that it charges borrowers for insurance by an additional 0.1 percentage points. This means that, when this change becomes effective, the annual premiums for most loans that are shown in **Table 3** will increase, depending on the loan-to-value ratio, to 1.3% (from 1.2%) or to 1.35% (from 1.25%), respectively.

Second, FHA plans to re-institute a policy of requiring borrowers to pay the annual mortgage insurance premium for the life of the loan. Currently, FHA follows a policy instituted in 2001 of canceling the mortgage insurance premium when the loan-to-value ratio reaches 78%, provided that the borrower has paid the premium for at least five years.[81] FHA notes that it continues to insure the entire loan amount even after the loan-to-value ratio reaches 78%, and that it has had to pay claims for loans for which borrowers were no longer paying mortgage insurance premiums.

Third, FHA announced that it plans to implement policies to encourage or require more borrowers of FHA-insured loans to receive housing counseling, which could improve the ability of these borrowers to stay current on their mortgages.[82] Details of such policies will be announced in the future.

---

[80] See FHA Mortgagee Letter 2012-22, released November 16, 2012, for more detailed information on these changes.

[81] The policy of canceling annual mortgage insurance premiums when the loan-to-value ratio reached 78% was established in FHA Mortgagee Letter 00-38, available at http://portal.hud.gov/hudportal/HUD?src=/program_offices/administration/hudclips/letters/mortgagee/2000ml. For loans where the mortgage term was fifteen years or less, borrowers could have their annual mortgage insurance premiums when the loan-to-value ratio reached 78% even if they had not been paying premiums for at least five years.

[82] For more information on housing counseling, see CRS Report R41351, *Housing Counseling: Background and Federal Role*, by Katie Jones.

Selected Legislative Proposals

Several policymakers have proposed making legislative changes to FHA's single-family program aimed at strengthening the MMI Fund's financial position and minimizing its risk. Some of these changes could also have the effect of reducing FHA's role in the mortgage market. This section briefly describes some recent legislative proposals related to the financial health of the MMI Fund, although it does not discuss all recent legislative debates related to FHA; for example, it does not discuss legislative proposals related to the FHA loan limits.

Some legislative changes that have been proposed to protect the MMI Fund include tightening underwriting standards for FHA-insured mortgages, such as increasing the required downpayment amount or raising the minimum credit score for borrowers seeking FHA-insured mortgages. Such changes could reduce the risk of borrowers defaulting on their mortgages, but could also have the effect of making some borrowers unable to qualify for FHA-insured mortgages. Other changes that have been suggested include allowing or requiring further increases in the mortgage insurance premiums charged to borrowers. (Because FHA is currently charging less than the maximum premium amounts allowed by law, FHA currently has the authority to increase its premiums further. However, legislation could require FHA to raise its premiums, or could raise the statutory maximums without requiring an increase in the premiums that are actually charged.)

Other suggested changes focus on providing FHA with additional authority to take actions against FHA-approved lenders who originate loans that do not conform to FHA's requirements. Namely, these proposals would expand FHA's authority to require lenders to compensate FHA under certain circumstances if the lenders originated FHA-insured mortgages that did not meet FHA's standards, and would expand FHA's authority to terminate lenders' approval to originate FHA-insured mortgages under certain circumstances. FHA has requested legislation to provide it with these expanded authorities.

Another set of suggested policy changes would require greater transparency and reporting from FHA on the performance of its insured mortgages, particularly during periods when the capital ratio is below 2%. For example, some have proposed requiring more frequent actuarial reports on the MMI Fund. Still other proposals would replace the Chief Risk Officer with a Deputy Secretary of HUD in charge of risk management for FHA.

Some of these proposed changes have been included in various bills that have been considered, but not enacted, in recent Congresses. In the 112th Congress, the FHA Emergency Fiscal Solvency Act of 2012 (H.R. 4264) was passed by the House of Representatives in September 2012 and includes some of the above provisions. Among other things, H.R. 4264 would do the following:

- it would raise both the minimum and maximum statutory annual mortgage insurance premiums that FHA can charge (the minimum premium would be set at 0.55%, a level that is below the annual mortgage insurance premium that FHA is currently charging);

- it would provide FHA with increased authority to terminate lenders' FHA approval and to require compensation from lenders under certain circumstances when mortgages do not meet FHA's requirements;

- it would create the position of Deputy Assistant Secretary for Risk Management and Regulatory Affairs within HUD;

- it would require greater reporting on the financial status of the MMI Fund, such as requiring HUD to submit an emergency capital plan that describes how FHA plans to restore the MMI Fund to financial soundness; requiring semiannual independent actuarial studies of the MMI Fund during periods when the capital ratio requirement is not being met, and requiring HUD to analyze the feasibility of conducting independent actuarial reviews of the MMI Fund on a quarterly basis; and requiring the Government Accountability Office (GAO) to provide for a one-time third-party review of the financial soundness of the MMI Fund conducted in accordance with generally accepted accounting principles.

A bill identical to the House bill (S. 3678) was introduced in the Senate in December 2012.

A number of additional bills containing various FHA reform provisions were introduced in the 112th Congress and other recent Congresses, but most of these bills were not reported out of committee.

Appendix. Annual Actuarial Review of the MMI Fund

By law, FHA is required to contract with an independent actuarial firm each year to analyze the actuarial soundness of the MMI Fund.[83] This annual actuarial review, which was discussed more briefly in the body of this report, is separate from the budgetary treatment of FHA-insured loans. This appendix describes the actuarial review and important related concepts, including the 2% capital ratio requirement, in more detail, and discusses the results of the FY2012 actuarial review released in November 2012.

In the annual actuarial review, the independent actuary reviews the MMI Fund's financial information to estimate the MMI Fund's current financial position, including the amount of funds it currently has on hand and the losses that it expects to incur in the future on the loans that it currently insures. It also uses economic modeling to project the MMI Fund's financial status for several years into the future under a "base case" scenario, based on current projections of future economic conditions, and several alternative economic scenarios. Some of the key terms used in the actuarial report include the following:

- *Capital resources* are the net assets (assets[84] minus liabilities) that the MMI Fund *currently* has on hand that can be converted into cash to pay claims on defaulted mortgages or other expenses.

- *Present value of future cash flows on outstanding business* is the estimated amount that the MMI Fund is currently expected to gain or lose in the future on the loans that it currently insures (this estimate does not take into account any new loans that might be insured in the future).

- *Economic value* is the difference between the MMI Fund's capital resources and the present value of future cash flows on outstanding business. It represents the amount of capital resources that the MMI Fund would have after expected future cash flows on currently insured loans are realized. In other words, it represents the amount that the MMI Fund currently has on hand that could be used to pay for any additional, unexpected losses on its outstanding loans.

In the FY2012 actuarial review,[85] the independent actuaries estimated the MMI Fund's total capital resources to be $30.4 billion (including both regular single-family mortgages and reverse mortgages). This is the amount of resources that FHA currently has on hand that can be converted into cash to pay claims. The actuaries estimated the present value of future cash flows on insured

---

[83] This requirement is codified at 12 U.S.C. 1708(a)(4). It was enacted as part of the Omnibus Budget Reconciliation Act of 1990 (P.L. 101-508) and the Cranston-Gonzalez National Affordable Housing Act of 1990 (P.L. 101-625). (Both laws included identical provisions related to the actuarial soundness of the MMI Fund.)

[84] The MMI Fund's assets include things such as cash, Treasury investments, and foreclosed properties held by HUD.

[85] There are actually two actuarial reviews: one analyzes only traditional FHA-insured single-family mortgages, and the other analyzes only FHA-insured reverse mortgages. Both of these actuarial reviews can be found at http://portal.hud.gov/hudportal/HUD?mode=dispcontent&id=HSG_ACTRMENU_10941&type=HUDGOV_HTML& rsm=Latest&width=664. FHA combines the numbers from the two actuarial reviews to arrive at a total economic value of the MMI Fund in its annual report to Congress on the status of the MMI Fund, which can be found at http://portal.hud.gov/hudportal/documents/huddoc?id=F12MMIFundRepCong111612.pdf. The discussion of the economic value of the MMI Fund and the capital ratio estimate begins on p. 34 of that report.

---

loans to be negative $46.6 billion. In other words, in present value terms, the loans that FHA currently insures are expected to cost FHA nearly $47 billion over the remaining life of those loans. The economic value of the MMI Fund, therefore, was estimated by the actuaries to be *negative* $16.3 billion ($30.4 billion - $46.6 billion). This is a decrease from an economic value of *positive* $2.6 billion at the end of FY2011, at which point the MMI Fund was estimated to have capital resources of $32.4 billion and a present value of future cash flows of negative $29.9 billion.[86] This represents the first time that the MMI Fund has been estimated to have a negative economic value since the early 1990s,[87] when a series of changes were enacted aimed at ensuring the financial soundness of the MMI Fund, including the requirement for an independent annual actuarial review.

A negative economic value means that the MMI Fund does not currently have enough capital resources on hand to pay for all of its expected future losses over the life of the loans that are currently insured. An economic value of negative $16.3 billion means that, based on the MMI Fund's current capital resources and current estimates of future cash flows on insured loans, FHA would be short about $16.3 billion when these currently insured loans ran their course. However, this does not mean that FHA is currently out of money.[88] The projected losses on the loans currently insured by FHA will be realized over the life of those loans, rather than all at once, potentially giving FHA time to increase its capital resources before these projected losses are realized. Whether or not the MMI Fund will ever actually run out of money to pay claims depends on factors such as whether the projections of future cash flows are accurate and whether the MMI Fund is able to build enough additional capital resources over time, such as through additional premium revenue from newly insured mortgages, to pay for these expected claims.

The projections included in the actuarial report rely on several assumptions. For one thing, the estimates of the MMI Fund's current status assume that FHA will not insure any more mortgages. In actuality, FHA will likely continue to insure loans, which will bring in new capital resources in the form of premium revenues, but will also create new liabilities in terms of claims.

Furthermore, the review relies upon assumptions about future economic conditions. To the extent that actual future economic conditions differ from these assumptions, the estimates of the MMI Fund's value will also be different.[89] Although the independent actuaries estimate that the MMI

---

[86] U.S. Department of Housing and Urban Development, *Annual Report to Congress Regarding the Financial Status of the FHA Mutual Mortgage Insurance Fund, Fiscal Year 2010*, p. 13, http://portal.hud.gov/hudportal/documents/huddoc?id=fhammifannrptfy2010.pdf.

[87] See, for example, General Accounting Office, *Mortgage Financing: Actuarial Soundness of the Federal Housing Administration's Mutual Mortgage Insurance Fund*, statement of Thomas J. McCool before the Subcommittee on Housing and Community Opportunity, House Committee on Financial Services, March 20, 2001, p. 2, showing an estimated negative economic value of the MMI Fund in 1990 and 1991.

[88] The FY2012 actuarial review estimates that there is about a 5% chance of the MMI Fund's capital resources becoming negative at some point in the next seven years. Negative capital resources would mean that FHA did not have money to pay current claims. See p. iii of the FY2012 actuarial review.

[89] To understand how assumptions about future economic conditions affect estimates of the MMI Fund's current value, consider that, for example, the *future* path of house prices affects *current* estimates of future cash flows on mortgages insured under the MMI Fund. If house prices fall more than expected in the future, then cash flows on currently insured mortgages might be more negative than currently anticipated due to more foreclosures and foreclosed properties held by FHA selling for less money; if house prices rise more than expected in the future, then cash flows on currently insured mortgages might be more positive than currently anticipated due to fewer foreclosures and foreclosed properties selling for more money. Likewise, assumptions about other economic indicators in the future also impact current estimates of future cash flows associated with currently insured mortgages.

Fund's economic value in FY2012 is negative $16 billion, they note that, under a variety of alternative future economic scenarios, the MMI Fund's economic value could be different. The actuaries estimated the MMI Fund's economic value under 100 randomly generated economic paths; the base case estimate (the negative $16 billion) represents the average expected economic value among these 100 paths. The base case estimate for traditional single-family mortgages only (excluding reverse mortgages) is negative $13.5 billion. Under the tenth-best economic scenario, the economic value for traditional single-family mortgages is actually positive in FY2012; under the worst scenario, the economic value is negative $65 billion.[90] Under two additional scenarios that were considered, a protracted economic slump scenario and a scenario where interest rates are lower for a longer period of time, the economic value would be more negative than is currently estimated. Under the protracted slump scenario, the economic value of the traditional single-family mortgages would remain negative through FY2019; under the low interest rate scenario, the economic value would become positive again in FY2015.

There are several reasons that the estimate of the MMI Fund's economic value is worse in FY2012 than it was in FY2011. One reason is updated interest rate and house price forecasts that are less favorable than the previous year. Another reason is a number of changes to the actuarial model, including some that were recommended by the Government Accountability Office (GAO) and others. A number of additional factors also contributed to changes in the estimate of the MMI Fund's economic value.[91]

The 2% Capital Ratio Requirement

In the Omnibus Budget Reconciliation Act of 1990 (P.L. 101-508), in response to concerns about the solvency of the FHA single-family insurance program, Congress mandated that, going forward, the MMI Fund's economic value must be at least 2% of the total dollar amount of loans[92] that it is currently insuring. This is known as the capital ratio requirement.[93] The capital ratio, then, is an expression of the economic value of the MMI Fund as a percentage of the total dollar volume of loans insured by the MMI Fund. It is a measure of how much capital the MMI Fund has on hand to pay for *unexpected* losses on currently insured loans, after the amounts estimated to be needed to cover *expected* losses are taken into account.

Brief History of the Capital Ratio Requirement

The capital ratio requirement for the MMI Fund was enacted by Congress in 1990 amid concerns that the Fund could become insolvent. In 1990, the MMI Fund had a negative economic value.

---

[90] U.S. Department of Housing and Urban Development, *Annual Report to Congress on the Financial Status of the MMI Fund, FY2012*, p. 47, http://portal.hud.gov/hudportal/documents/huddoc?id=F12MMIFundRepCong111612.pdf.

[91] See pages 20-27 of the FY2012 actuarial review for more information on the factors that accounted for changes in the economic value of the MMI Fund and the impact of each of these factors.

[92] The legislation calls for the capital ratio to be calculated as the economic value of the MMI Fund divided by unamortized insurance-in-force. Unamortized insurance-in-force is generally understood to mean the original principal balance of insured mortgages. However, the legislation defines unamortized insurance-in-force as "the remaining obligation on outstanding mortgages," a definition that is usually understood to be amortized insurance-in-force. The actuarial report includes both amortized and unamortized insurance-in-force as generally understood, allowing the capital ratio to be calculated both ways.

[93] 12 U.S.C. 1711(f). The Omnibus Budget Reconciliation Act of 1990 is also the law that required annual independent actuarial reports on the Mutual Mortgage Insurance Fund.

This meant that the expected future cash flows associated with the mortgages currently insured by the MMI Fund were higher than the capital resources that the Fund had on hand to pay for those claims. In response, legislation passed by Congress directed FHA to make certain changes that were intended to result in the Fund building up reserves of at least 2% of the dollar volume of mortgages that it currently insured to cover future unexpected losses on these insured loans. These changes included charging borrowers an annual mortgage insurance premium to go along with the existing premium that was paid upfront and suspending certain payments, known as distributive shares, that were previously paid to borrowers under certain conditions. The law also established the requirement for the annual independent actuarial review. Some of these changes, such as the additional mortgage insurance premium, essentially meant that FHA would charge more to future borrowers to build up reserves to pay for losses on mortgages made to past borrowers.

As Congress considered the legislation, there was debate over the appropriate level for the capital ratio requirement.[94] This debate highlights the ongoing tension that FHA faces between maintaining its financial soundness and carrying out its purpose of expanding access to affordable mortgage credit for underserved borrowers. The 2% threshold was adopted because it was viewed as being high enough to provide FHA with a cushion to withstand unexpected losses, but without imposing an undue financial burden on future FHA-insured borrowers. A higher capital ratio requirement would have likely required FHA to charge higher premiums for FHA insurance. It was recognized that a 2% requirement would likely be high enough to withstand moderate future economic downturns, but would likely not be high enough to allow the MMI Fund to withstand a catastrophic economic downturn. According to GAO testimony from 2000:

> Determining what constitutes an adequate reserve level is essentially a question of what kinds of adverse economic conditions—moderately severe or catastrophic—the reserve should be able to withstand.... In the actuarial review of the Fund conducted by Price Waterhouse for fiscal year 1989, the researchers concluded that actuarial soundness would be consistent with a reserve that could withstand adverse, but not catastrophic, economic downturns. They further concluded that the Treasury implicitly covers catastrophic risk.... By contrast, rating agencies have taken the position, when evaluating private mortgage insurers, that they should have enough capital to withstand catastrophic risk.... However, requiring FHA to hold capital equivalent to that held by private mortgage insurers would likely impair FHA's public purpose.[95]

While the law requires the Secretary of HUD to ensure that the MMI Fund maintains a capital ratio of 2%, it does not specify consequences or specific actions that the Secretary must take if the capital ratio falls below that threshold.[96]

---

[94] See the discussion of the history of the capital ratio in Capone Jr., Charles A., "Credit Risk, Capital, and Federal Housing Administration Mortgage Insurance," Journal of Housing Research, Volume 11, Issue 2, available at http://content.knowledgeplex.org/kp2/img/cache/kp/1215.pdf.

[95] United States General Accounting Office, *Mortgage Financing: Financial Health of the Federal Housing Administration's Mutual Mortgage Insurance Fund*, Statement of Stanley J. Czerwinski before the Subcommittee on Housing and Transportation, Senate Committee on Banking, Housing and Urban Affairs, September 12, 2000, p. 7-8, http://gao.gov/assets/110/108623.pdf.

[96] The capital ratio requirement is codified at 12 U.S.C. § 1711(f). A separate section of the law, 12 U.S.C. § 1708(a)(3), also requires the Secretary to make sure that the MMI Fund is financially sound.

The Capital Ratio in Recent Years

The capital ratio is reported in FHA's annual report to Congress on the status of the MMI Fund, using the actuarial report's numbers for both traditional single-family mortgages and reverse mortgages insured by FHA. In FY2009, the capital ratio was estimated to be 0.53%,[97] representing the first time that the capital ratio had fallen below 2% since the requirement was first met in FY1995.[98] The capital ratio has remained below 2% since then.

As noted, the independent actuarial report estimated the economic value of the MMI Fund to be negative $16.3 billion in FY2012. The MMI Fund included about $1.1 trillion in insured mortgages at the end of FY2012. The capital ratio, therefore, was estimated to be *negative* 1.44% (negative $16.3 billion divided by $1.1 trillion). This is the first time that the economic value of the MMI Fund, and by extension the capital ratio, has been negative since the capital ratio requirement was first met.

A negative capital ratio signals a negative economic value of the MMI Fund. As described earlier, a negative economic value indicates that the MMI Fund does not currently have enough capital resources on hand to cover the losses it expects to incur over the life of the loans that it currently insures. This suggests that the MMI Fund could at some point need to draw on its permanent and indefinite budget authority with Treasury in order to have enough funds on hand to cover all of its future expected losses. It does not mean that the MMI Fund has run out of money at this point in time.

A negative capital ratio by itself does not trigger any special assistance from Treasury, although it suggests that such assistance could be needed at some point. Rather, any special assistance from Treasury would be triggered if the credit subsidy rate re-estimate process described in the "Credit Subsidy Rate Re-estimates" section showed that FHA needed more funds than it had on hand to hold against expected losses on the loans that it currently insures. The amount of special assistance required would be based on the credit subsidy rate re-estimates, not on the capital ratio or the economic value of the MMI Fund as reported in the actuarial report.

Table 5 shows the MMI Fund's actuarial position, including its economic value, dollar volume of insured mortgages, and capital ratio, as estimated by the independent actuaries for each fiscal year between FY2006 and FY2012.

---

[97] U.S. Department of Housing and Urban Development, *Annual Report to Congress Regarding the Financial Status of the Mutual Mortgage Insurance Fund, FY2009*, November 12, 2009, p. 17, http://portal.hud.gov/hudportal/documents/huddoc?id=fhammifannrptfy2009.pdf. This capital ratio uses amortized insurance-in-force, as generally understood, as the denominator of the ratio.

[98] U.S. Department of Housing and Urban Development, Office of Policy Development and Research, "The FHA Single-Family Insurance Program: Performing a Needed Role in the Housing Finance Market," Executive Summary, p. 3, http://www.huduser.org/publications/pdf/FHA_SingleFamilyIns_2012.pdf. The discussion of the history of FHA notes that the capital ratio requirement of 2% was first reached in FY1995.

Table 5. MMI Fund's Actuarial Position, FY2006-FY2012

$ in millions

	Capital Resources	PV of Future Cash Flows	Economic Value	Dollar Volume of Insured Mortgages	Capital Ratio
FY2006	$23,461	-$1,440	$22,021	$298,542	7.38%
FY2007	$25,365	-$3,952	$21,277	$305,449	6.97%
FY2008	$27,281	-$14,374	$12,908	$401,461	3.22%
FY2009	$30,719	-$27,078	$3,641	$684,708	0.53%
FY2010	$33,594	-$28,937	$4,657	$931,272	0.50%
FY2011	$32,431	-$29,880	$2,551	$1,078,000	0.24%
FY2012	$30,362	-$46,638	-$16,277	$1,131,543	-1.44%

Source: FHA's Annual Reports to Congress on the Financial Status of the MMI Fund

Notes: Figures are based on the base case scenario reported in the actuarial reports. FHA-insured reverse mortgages became part of the MMI Fund in FY2009.

The drop in the capital ratio in recent years is the result of both a decrease in the numerator of the ratio (the MMI Fund's economic value) and an increase in the denominator of the ratio (total dollar volume of mortgages outstanding), which reflects the fact that FHA is insuring a greater volume of loans than it has in the recent past. The decrease in the MMI Fund's economic value, in turn, is mostly due to the fact that the present value of future cash flows has been increasingly negative, suggesting that FHA is currently expecting large net cash outflows over the life of the loans that it currently insures.

Projections of the MMI Fund's Future Financial Position

In addition to estimating the MMI Fund's current economic value, the actuarial review also estimates the MMI Fund's projected economic value and capital ratio for several years into the future. (While the estimates of the MMI Fund's current actuarial position assume that FHA will not insure any more loans in the future, estimates of the MMI Fund's future value do take into account the amount that mortgages insured in the future are expected to earn or lose for the MMI Fund.) Based on the independent actuarial report, FHA estimates that, under its base case scenario, the MMI Fund is projected to regain a positive capital ratio in FY2014, and to regain a capital ratio of 2% in FY2017.[99] However, as noted earlier, such estimates rely on a number of assumptions. If these assumptions are not realized—for example, if house prices are lower than expected, or if more recent loans insured by FHA do not perform as well as anticipated—then it could take several more years before the capital ratio regains a level of 2.0%.

Table 6 shows the projections of the capital ratio in each year from FY2013 through FY2019 under the base case scenario, based on the actuarial report. It also shows the projected economic value (the numerator of the capital ratio) and the projected dollar amount of outstanding insurance (the denominator of the capital ratio) in each of those years. The FY2012 actuarial report

---

[99] U.S. Department of Housing and Urban Development, *Annual Report to Congress on the Financial Status FHA Mutual Mortgage Insurance Fund, Fiscal Year 2012*, November 16, 2012, pp. 36, http://portal.hud.gov/hudportal/documents/huddoc?id=F12MMIFundRepCong111612.pdf.

estimates that, under the base case scenario, the MMI Fund's economic value will increase over each of the next several years, reaching nearly $54 billion by FY2019. However, these estimates are less favorable than those in the FY2011 actuarial review, which had suggested that the MMI Fund could have economic values of positive $11.5 billion in FY2012, $27.7 billion in FY2013, and almost $70 billion by FY2018. The corresponding capital ratio estimates in the FY2011 actuarial review were 1% in FY2012, 1.56% in FY2013, and 4% in FY2018. The FY2011 actuarial review had anticipated that the MMI Fund would regain a capital ratio of 2% in FY2014 under the base case scenario assumptions.

Table 6. Projections of MMI Fund Capital Ratio in the Future, FY2012-FY2019

$ in millions

	Economic Value	Dollar Volume of Insured Mortgages	Capital Ratio
FY2012	-$16, 300	$1,131,000	-1.4%
FY2013	-$5,300	$1,230,000	-0.4%
FY2014	$2,000	$1,291,000	0.2%
FY2015	$9,700	$1,314,000	0.7%
FY2016	$19,700	$1,352,000	1.5%
FY2017	$30,700	$1,401,000	2.2%
FY2018	$42,000	$1,441,000	2.9%
FY2019	$53,900	$1,467,000	3.7%

Source: FHA Annual Report to Congress on the Financial Status of the MMI Fund, FY2012, p. 36.

Notes: Figures are based on the base case scenario reported in the actuarial reports.

Estimates of the Fund's economic value in future years largely rely on estimates of the economic value of the cohorts of loans expected to be insured in future years. For example, the estimate of the MMI Fund's economic value in FY2018 includes estimates of the economic value of the loans that are expected to be insured in each fiscal year from FY2013 to FY2019. The actuarial report projects that the cohorts of traditional single-family loans (excluding reverse mortgages) insured in each of those fiscal years will have positive economic values ranging between about $6.8 (in FY2014) billion and $10.9 billion (in FY2013).[100] The actuarial review attributes this largely to fewer FHA-insured loans refinancing out of FHA mortgages to conventional mortgages as interest rates begin to rise, and FHA continuing to insure high dollar volumes of new loans each year.[101] Loans insured in recent or future years could also potentially perform better due to better credit quality of newly insured mortgages, higher insurance premiums, and the end of seller-funded downpayment assistance loans.

The independent actuaries estimate that the traditional single-family loans insured by FHA in FY2013 will have an economic value of nearly $11 billion. If this estimate is accurate, then that

---

[100] Integrated Financial Engineering, Inc., prepared for the U.S. Department of Housing and Urban Development, *Actuarial Review of the Federal Housing Administration Mutual Mortgage Insurance Fund Forward Loans for Fiscal Year 2012*, November 5, 2012, p. 36, available at http://portal.hud.gov/hudportal/HUD?mode=dispcontent&id=HSG_ACTRMENU_10941&type=HUDGOV_HTML&rsm=Latest&width=664.

[101] Ibid., p. 16.

could help reduce the likelihood that FHA will need to draw funds from Treasury to cover higher expected future losses. If the assumptions of the actuaries turn out to be incorrect, however, and the economic value of new loans insured by FHA is lower than expected, then FHA would have a higher likelihood of needing to draw funds from Treasury at some point. The economic value of loans insured in future years could be lower than estimated for several reasons. For example, if FHA insures a lower volume of loans than anticipated, it could bring in less premium revenue than it currently expects. If the credit quality of the loans is not as good as anticipated, then default rates would likely be higher than expected, and the economic value would be lower. If interest rates or house prices follow substantially different paths than those expected under the base case scenario, then mortgages insured going forward might not bring in as much premium revenue as expected or might result in more claim losses than currently anticipated.

Author Contact Information

Katie Jones
Analyst in Housing Policy
kmjones@crs.loc.gov, 7-4162